Information Technology
and the Productivity Paradox

Information Technology
and the Productivity Paradox

ASSESSING THE VALUE
OF INVESTING IN IT

Henry C. Lucas, Jr.

New York   Oxford
Oxford University Press
1999

Oxford University Press

Oxford   New York
Athens   Auckland   Bangkok   Bogotá   Buenos Aires   Calcutta   Cape Town   Chennai
Dar es Salaam   Delhi   Florence   Hong Kong   Istanbul   Karachi   Kuala Lumpur
Madrid   Melbourne   Mexico City   Mumbai   Nairobi   Paris   São Paulo   Singapore
Taipei   Tokyo   Toronto   Warsaw

and associated companies in

Berlin   Ibadan

Copyright © 1999 by Oxford University Press, Inc.

Published by Oxford University Press, Inc.,
198 Madison Avenue, New York, New York 10016

Oxford is a registered trademark of Oxford University Press

Library of Congress Cataloging-in-Publication Data
Lucas, Henry C.
    Information technology and the productivity paradox : assessing the value of
investing in IT / by Henry C. Lucas, Jr.
        p. cm.
    Includes bibliographical references and index.
    ISBN 0–19–512159–7 (alk. paper)
    1. Information technology—Finance. 2. Capital investments.
3. Rate of return. I. Title.
HC79.I55L83   1999
658.4'038—dc21   98–21470

9 8 7 6 5 4 3 2 1

Printed in the United States of America
on acid-free paper

TO: ELLEN

CONTENTS

PREFACE

Do today's massive investments in information technology (IT) produce value? Are the technologists who argue that technology can solve any problem right, or are the skeptics who think that corporations are wasting vast sums on IT correct? I believe that information technology is an integral part of competing in the twenty-first century, and the objective of this book is to demonstrate that there is value from investing in IT.

Academic studies present conflicting results on the value of information technology. Companies continue to invest large sums in IT; we shall see examples of firms with IT budgets in excess of $1 billion per year. One might argue these companies must feel they get a return from this investment, or they would not make it. Yet, business history is replete with fads, programs that companies undertake because other companies are doing the same thing and they do not want to be left behind. In the past decade we have gone through total quality management, expert systems, and reengineering, to name a few. Could IT be such a fad? Are organizations investing simply because they see other companies implementing new technology?

My personal belief is that information technology produces substantial value, but that value has many different dimensions. Value is not synonymous with ROI; there are more kinds of value than a measurable financial return on investment. One of the purposes of this book is to identify different ways in which IT produces value. We will examine the evidence for different types of value and explore ways to make decisions about investments in IT. I believe that firms which invest wisely in information technology and turn their investments into successful applications will be the leaders in the competitive economy of the twenty-first century.

Part I of the book sets the stage for discussing evidence about the value from IT investments. Chapter 1 presents the Investment Opportunities Matrix, a framework for classifying different kinds of IT initiatives. The matrix indicates which kinds of IT investments are most likely to show a return, and the type of return one might expect from them. Chapter 2 presents a "garbage can model" of information technology. It emphasizes the importance of conversion effectiveness, turning an investment into a successful application, in obtaining value from IT investments. This chapter presents two fundamental equations: the IT Investment Equation and the IT Value Equation.

Part II of the book begins the search for value from different types of IT investments introduced in the first chapter. In Chapter 3, we look at studies of multiple companies to see if there is evidence for a return from IT at the industry or at an aggregate level. Chapter 4 presents examples of direct, measurable returns from IT; it discusses the type of system where one is most likely to be able to compute a positive return on investment. It provides the strongest evidence that IT investments can yield financial value.

Part III discusses indirect and less obvious returns from technology. Chapter 5 introduces a new category of IT initiative, one that shows an indirect return. This kind of return is probably not anticipated when the organization decides on an IT investment, but it has the potential to be larger than any direct returns. Chapter 6 deals with investments in IT infrastructure. These initiatives may not have a return in the near term; their payoff is likely to come in the future. Chapter 7 presents examples where information technology has become a part of corporate strategy, providing a potentially large return. However, with IT it is hard to sustain a competitive advantage because a competitor can easily copy your initiative. This chapter also delves into the kind of IT investment that is a competitive necessity, such as ATMs for a bank. Chapter 8 discusses how IT investments can enable organization transformations; it shows how five companies have used IT design variables to create different kinds of responsive and highly competitive organization structures.

Part IV focuses on improving the chances for successful IT initiatives. Chapter 9 discusses ways to improve conversion effectiveness, the process of converting an IT investment into a functioning application. Chapter 10 draws on the previous chapters to offer advice on making IT investments. It discusses the role of net present value and options pricing models in providing information for the decision maker. The chapter suggests a format for structuring IT investment decisions along with an approach to evaluating each initiative in the IT portfolio.

Part V is devoted to the implications of the discussion so far. Chapter 11 presents a framework for managing information technology. Management needs a vision and plan to help guide IT investment decisions. Approaches to the management of IT and the role of the CIO are all part of the environment for making IT investment decisions. Chapter 12 summarizes our search for IT value and reviews the evidence in the book. While there is always room for more and stronger evidence, we conclude that managers can make effective decisions about investments in information technology that create value for the organization.

I would like to acknowledge permission to include Table 4-1 and a condensed version of our paper on the Merrill Lynch SPC system from the Association for Computing Machinery in Chapter 4. I acknowledge permission to use Table 4-2 from Benaroche and Kauffman, (forthcoming) from INFORMS. McGraw-Hill gave permission to use material in Chapter 5 on strategic IT and the discussion of IT management in Chapter 11 from my book *Information Technology for Management* (6th ed.) (1997). Jossey-Bass provided permission to summarize some of the examples of organizational transformation in Chapter 8 taken from my book *The T-Form Organization: Using Technology to Design Organizations for the 21st Century* (1996). *Sloan Management Review* gave permission to reprint Tables 11-1, 11-2, and 11-3 from Earl and Feeny.

I also acknowledge helpful conversations about the contents of the book with Ted Stohr, Bruce Weber, Raghu Garud, and Yakov Amihud of the Stern School, New York University. I am also indebted to Katherine Duliba and Wonseok Oh for their reviews of the manuscript. I would like to thank Herb Addison, business editor for Oxford University Press, for his encouragement and support of the book. Finally, I am indebted to my wife, Ellen, for 30 years of understanding the idiosyncrasies of someone who writes occasional books and articles.

Information Technology
and the Productivity Paradox

PART I

Introduction and the Garbage Can Model

The first two chapters of the book put forward arguments that are crucial for finding value from investments in information technology. An important point is that the value the firm receives depends on the type of IT investment it makes. Chapter 1 presents an Investment Opportunities Matrix, which categorizes different types of IT investments and describes the kind of return, if any, one can expect from them. The chapter introduces the crucial notion that there is uncertainty associated with the value from IT, and that this uncertainty varies according to the type of technology investment.

The second chapter presents the garbage can model of IT value. While an unusual analogy, this model illustrates the challenges of obtaining a return from IT investments. The garbage can holds a number of actors and technologies. The spigot from the can leads to IT value, but a number of projects leak out on the way. The chapter introduces the idea of conversion effectiveness, the ability of the firm to turn an IT investment into a successful application. The chapter also presents two equations, the *IT Investment Equation* and the *IT Value Equation,* which help us understand the likelihood of obtaining a return from IT investments and the expected magnitude of that return.

CHAPTER ONE

Is it Reasonable to Expect a Return from Investments in Information Technology?

What is the value of investments in information technology (IT)? Is there a return from investing in IT? These two questions are critical because firms invest huge amounts in information technology; an estimated 50 percent of U.S. capital investment today is for IT. For top-ranked banks like Chase and Citibank, express carriers like FedEx and UPS, and large brokerage firms, annual IT budgets approach or exceed $1 billion. The chairman of NationsBank, Hugh McColl, stated at a CEO series seminar at New York University in April 1997 that his bank was spending $500 million a year on software and had a total IT budget of *$1.9 billion*. After its merger with Bank of America, the combined banks will initially have an annual IT budget of $4 billion! (Only a portion of these budgets represents investment in new IT initiatives; the rest is for ongoing operations.)

Obtaining value from IT is important for organizations to survive and flourish in the highly competitive economy of the twenty-first century. Many of us believe that information technology holds the key to success as companies develop systems that provide them with a competitive advantage. IT also lets managers create dynamic, new organization structures to compete more effectively. Firms that create value through information technology will be the winners in the coming century.

The fundamental premise of this book is that there is value from information technology, and that it is possible to show a return from certain kinds of investments in IT. It is important to understand *under what conditions one can expect to find a measurable return from IT investments.* We also need to find creative ways to *measure* IT value. If we can accomplish these two tasks, it should be possible to predict what investments will lead to a return, and the nature of that return.

The purpose of this book, then, is to

- present a perspective on the nature of the value from investing in IT;

- demonstrate that there have been and should continue to be returns from IT investments: there is value to be found in information technology;

- suggest ways to look for both the obvious and the more subtle value from IT;

- make recommendations on how to evaluate proposed investments in technology.

What Is Value?

This is a book about the search for value from investing in information technology, but what is value? The most common meaning of value is monetary worth; in the marketplace buyers and sellers place a value on goods and services that is measured in dollars. When an investor seeks a return on capital, it is expressed as a percentage of the original investment. However, the term "value" sometimes has a very remote connection with money; for example, a manager describes an employee who makes a valuable contribution to the firm. It might be possible to trace this contribution to the company's profits, but that is not the intent of the comment.

Because information technology is woven into the fabric of business, this book adopts a broad definition of the value of IT investments. The marketplace establishes prices, and the most familiar measure of value from investing in technology is dollars returned. As we shall see, computing a monetary value for a return from IT investments is not easy. In fact, in some cases, it almost appears impossible, at least at the time the firm is making the investment.

A good example is investing in IT infrastructure; a company might invest heavily to build a network of computers; the return from that network comes in literally hundreds of ways, as individual employees use the network to do their jobs better and IT staff members build applications of technology that take advantage of the network infrastructure. At the time the firm decided to invest in the network, it could only guess at the nature of activities the network might stimulate. A few years later, it is possible to study the return on the projects the network enabled, but it is a rare company that would devote the time and resources to such a post hoc analysis.

In searching for IT value, we seek all types of contributions from investments in technology. Some investments demonstrate traditional returns that can be expressed in monetary terms. Other examples demonstrate indirect returns from IT investments. Sometimes, it appears that an IT investment has prevented a negative return, for example, when a firm develops a system to keep up with a competitor and avoid losing market share. In instances where technology becomes intertwined with the strategy of the corporation, the contribution of IT seems very valuable but exceedingly difficult to value.

Consider Morgan Stanley, a leading investment bank and a major force in retail brokerage through its merger with Dean Witter in 1997. The investment bank's technology (without its new acquisition) is a 24-hour-per-day, seven-day-a-week operation. There are 15,000 computers used to process 100,000 trades a day. The firm has an estimated 100 million lines of software code and an Intranet with 10,000 users. Each night, its batch processing cycle executes 34,000 jobs. This kind of business requires a tremendous investment in technology. Has Morgan Stanley received a return on this investment? We shall try to answer questions like this in the rest of the book.

What Is Information Technology?

What makes information technology such a powerful force in the economy? Three components of IT—computers, databases, and communications networks—are transforming organizations, markets, and education. Information technology includes these three major components along with other devices like voice mail systems, fax machines, personal digital assistants like the Palm Pilot, and similar electronic devices that promote computation, storage, and the communication of data. Understanding a bit of history and the capabilities of modern IT sets the stage for a discussion of the value one might expect from investing in this technology.

The first electronic computers were developed during World War II for military applications. During the 1950s computers based on vacuum tube technology began to appear in businesses. By the 1960s most large companies used computers to process batch jobs, that is, applications where users submitted data, clerks punched the data into cards, and the computer ran the data to update computer files on tape or disk. The American Airlines SABRE system inaugurated on-line processing in business in the early 1960s. Toward the end of this decade and into the 1970s, on-line became the preferred method of working with computers. During this time period, companies led by Digital Equipment Corporation developed minicomputers, which were used almost exclusively in an on-line, interactive mode.

Although personal computers were around before 1981, this was the year that IBM unveiled its PC, legitimizing "small" computers as far as business customers were concerned. Over the next ten years, these computers became more powerful, as thousands of software companies developed programs for them. Users at first welcomed the idea of having their own computers, independent of a central information systems department. However, users soon found benefits in sharing programs and data, so local area networks were developed.

In 1969 the U.S. Defense Department sponsored the development of the ARPANET to connect various universities and Defense contractors. This wide area network grew over the next 20 years to become the Internet. The development of a graphical browser—Mosaic and then Netscape and then Internet Explorer—made the World Wide Web (WWW) available and easy to use on the Internet. When the National Science Foundation eliminated its support of the Internet in the early 1990s, the rules changed so that it could be used for profit-making activities. With this change, business began to use the Internet, and the Internet began a period of exponential growth.

We can divide the growth of information technology into three major eras, each with developments that changed the way business and commerce functioned. The first era is the development of the computer itself. The incredible speed of the computer made it possible to do tasks that could not be done manually. Imagine a group of people taking telephone calls for customers who want to make reservations on American Airlines; this group would have to process over 4,000 transactions *a second* during a peak, something the SABRE computers are capable of doing. The airlines also revise their fares daily to maximize revenue.

The second major era in technology brought the database. There are actually several components to databases:

Software or programs that facilitate the creation of the database and help organize it for storage and retrieval purposes

The data itself, which has to be created or converted into machine-readable form so that it can be stored in the database

High-capacity disk drives that alone can store billions of characters of data; companies use multiple disk drives to store terrabytes (trillions) of bytes of data

Data storage does not sound very exciting on the surface, but think about the implications of being able to store huge quantities of data, and then search and retrieve information of interest in a few seconds or less.

This technology lets a company like Frito-Lay record the sales of all of its products to customers at the level of the individual store. Local managers review sales to look for problems and to plan promotions. Added to these data is competitive information purchased from market research firms so that Frito-Lay can respond to the competition as well as to customer demand.

The third era of information technology added communications networks to the existing components. It is now possible to tie together computers and databases all over the world so that they can exchange data. In addition, because individuals have workstations (personal computers) on their desks, they can use the network to send and receive electronic mail (e-mail). *The combination of computers, databases, and networks has expanded the range of technology from purely computational to a powerful communications medium.*

Change usually takes a long time, and the technology that transformed organizations and the economy is no exception. Why should anyone be excited about the slow growth of information technology? It took mainframe computers a decade or two to become central to most firms. In fact, when IBM marketed its first mainframe computer, it estimated that 20 of these machines would fulfill the world's need for computation! Minicomputers moved into companies and schools a little faster than mainframes, but they were also considerably less expensive. Even the ubiquitous PC took five to ten years to become an important part of work life.

The Internet was an academic and research institution network for over 20 years before business discovered it. We have a new unit called "Internet Time," a measure that stands for extremely rapid response and short development cycles. After the Internet became available for profit-making activities, it began to grow exponentially. Networking experts feel that a new era of electronic commerce is approaching in which significant amounts of business will be conducted over the Internet.

As an example, Dell Computer has set up a Web site to accept orders. Within a short period of time, the company reached a level of $1 million *a day* in sales through this channel. As of this writing Dell's site records $6 million a day in sales and is accessed 800,000 times a week. Cisco, a company that makes network communications products that are in high demand in organizations building their networks and connecting to the Internet, set up a Web site to accept orders. Within six months, the company was selling equipment at the rate of $1 billion a year from the Web site. By the end of 1997, Cicso reported annual sales through the Internet of over $3 billion. Internet time also refers to the speed with which various companies develop products for the Net. When Bill Gates's Microsoft embraced the Internet, the company created a new division with 2,500 employees; in less than a year this division produced three releases of a browser, the Internet Explorer, and pulled almost even with Netscape, the market leader.

The financial markets reflect the explosion of technology in the economy. In the spring of 1997, Microsoft and Intel had a combined market value of $224.8 billion. This is more than the combined market values of General Motors, Ford, Boeing, Eastman Kodak, Sears, J. P. Morgan, Caterpillar and Kellogg! The reason for this is that investors probably see no limit on the future growth prospects for Intel and Microsoft and that there is no apparent upper bound on the technology. Sales of these other companies, however, are all constrained by market potential, environmental concerns, or the amount of capital available.

Today we are all confronted with an incredibly powerful technology that makes it possible to search vast amounts of data stored in locations around the world, a technology that offers services that could only have been imagined 20 years ago and has the potential to revolutionize the way we structure organizations and conduct commerce. But the question remains: *Has anyone obtained a return from investing in information technology?*

Challenging Conventional Wisdom and Practice

A large number of researchers have expressed concern because they cannot find a significant impact on productivity from the large investments organizations have made in information technology. In his article "Taking Computers to Task" (*Scientific American,* July 1997), W. Wayt Gibbs reports estimates that U.S. firms spent 43 percent of their capital budgets in 1996 on hardware alone, more than they invested in factories or any other type of durable equipment. Adding in software, networks and staff, the IT bill for 1996 is estimated at $500 billion in the United States and more than $1 trillion worldwide. The article questions whether these investments have shown up in productivity statistics. In a similar vein, an editorial in the Wall Street Journal (August 11, 1997) asks where the information technology payoff is, and suggests that any savings are offset by more government red tape!

Robert Solow, a Nobel laureate economist, is supposed to have said that "PCs are showing up all over the place, except in productivity statistics." In a 1993 article, Eric Brynjolfsson wrote about the "productivity paradox," the fact that the benefits of IT spending have not shown up in aggregate output statistics.

He offers two possible explanations. First, the results of IT spending occur locally and cannot be expected to show up in aggregate statistics at the national level. Second, the benefits from IT investment often require restructuring or major cost-cutting, and it is possible that firms have yet to undertake enough of this activity for it to be reflected in national statistics. There are also suggestions that the lack of finding of an impact of IT on national productivity is partly a measurement problem: The government tends to equate output to input in the services industry, where 7 out of 10 American workers are employed. A Stanford economist, Paul David, suggests that it took over 40 years after the first electric motor was installed before managers designed plants to take advantage of this technology; IT may exhibit the same phenomenon.

Questions about the national productivity impacts of information technology are interesting for economists to debate. What is their relevance to the individual manager? The manager investing in IT is interested in the value obtained in his or her organization, possibly even his or her subunit of that organization. While it would be nice for IT to have an impact on national productivity, our concern in this book is with value at the level of the firm and its subunits. We shall review some studies of multiple firms in Chapter 3 to see if they demonstrate value, and we will find that there is some evidence of a return on IT investments among groups of firms, if not at the level of national productivity.

The search for value from IT investments, particularly at the level of national productivity statistics, has an underlying philosophical belief that technology investments are a good thing, and that firms choose to invest in IT only if they believe there will be a positive return from their investment. There is also an implicit belief that the predicted benefits of an investment are realized after implementing new technology.

Two key points of this chapter are that *not all investments in IT should be expected to show a measurable return,* and *investments can have value to an organization even without demonstrable financial return.* In many organizations, there seems to be a strong belief that every investment is made with the expectation of a positive return. One reviewer of this book stated that his firm never undertook an IT investment without expecting benefits that exceeded its costs. Personal experience makes me wonder if his organization is typical.

A number of years ago I asked a manager in the field if his firm only undertook an application of technology when the benefits exceeded the cost of the project. He responded that this was definitely the case. I then asked, "What if you really feel that you want to develop the application, but you can't show benefits that exceed costs." He answered, "We add on enough intangible benefits (better decision-making is a popular one) to justify the investment."

More recently I had a panel of IT managers speaking to a class that I teach called Information Technology: Strategy and Management. I asked the panel if all of the projects they encountered were justified with a rigorous net present value analysis. No one on the panel raised a hand. After the laughter from the class died down (we had some debates on the topic during the semester), a consultant on the panel offered an example.

He had been involved in the tremendously successful MCI "Friends and Family" product. He asked the manager for this project what the information technology component was worth. The reply surprised him: "Zero." The MCI manager went on to explain that the advertising part of the project was also worth zero. Each of these components could not have worked without all the others. Together, the Friends and Family product was extremely successful. Individually, its components were not worth anything, but certainly the technology part of this initiative added value to the Friends and Family product. Situations like this make it very difficult to identify the return from investing in information technology. They also point out that the technology does not necessarily stand alone; it is an integral part of products and services in modern firms. A change of any kind in the organization today is likely to involve a new investment in technology.

A major brokerage firm determined that it needed to develop a new broker workstation for its retail business. Retail brokers were using outmoded technology, and the retail business unit felt that it needed a new system for several reasons. First, the firm needed to demonstrate to its customers that its brokers were well informed and had access to the latest technology. A second important reason was to retain brokers; other firms recruit this company's brokers, and brokers tend to take their clients with them when they move to a new company. Finally, the brokerage firm felt it could increase its business with the new system. The initial request for funding from the business unit and the IT group was around $750 million. A source in the company told me that the board of directors approved the request without an ROI estimate or any significant economic analysis. The retail business unit made an argument for the investment based on the need to stay competitive and on its ability to fund the project. They anticipated value from the workstation project and were willing to make a substantial investment in it. Currently the project is expected to exceed the original estimate by a significant amount, but no one in the firm seems worried by the overrun.

One of the most controversial statements in this book, then, is that *there are applications where you cannot expect to obtain a measurable financial return from investing in information technology.* There are times when you will invest without the expectation of a return regardless of company policy or mythology about never making an investment without a positive net present value, or without concrete, identifiable benefits exceeding costs.

The IT Investment Opportunities Matrix

There are many different reasons for investing in IT, and there are valid reasons for choosing not to undertake a project. Table 1-1 presents the Investment Opportunities Matrix, which attempts to place different kinds of information technology investments into perspective. The first column of the table describes the kind of investment in technology that one can undertake. The second column provides an example, and the third offers comments on this investment type. The fourth column, "upside," discusses the possibility that you will obtain a much larger return than predicted. An extraordinary return might result because an investment worked much better than expected, or a product with IT as a component became extremely popular, like the Merrill Lynch Cash Management Account in the 1980s or the more recent MCI Friends and Family program.

The last column in Table 1-1 provides an estimate of the probability that there will be a return from the investment in this type of system. If the estimated probability here is 0.5, that means there is a 50 percent chance that you will get a return from this type of investment. The column presents ranges because the return depends on the specific IT investment you are planning to make. The second number in the column is my estimate for what you can expect in general for an investment in this type of IT.

The probabilities in Table 1-1 are subjective; they are based on my estimate from having encountered a large number of applications and descriptions of IT investments. Providing numbers like this is controversial; my objective is not to convince the reader that a particular probability estimate is the correct number. *The point is that there is not the same likelihood of a return from each IT investment.* The reader is encouraged to supply his or her own numbers after reading more about the different types of investments. It may be easier to estimate the probability of a return for a specific IT investment under review than to provide estimates for the categories in Table 1-1.)

Infrastructure. Our transportation infrastructure consists of roads, interstate highways, rail lines, and airports to name a few components. Infrastructure tends to be expensive and not terribly exciting, but extremely important.

Table 1-1

IT Investment Opportunities Matrix

Type of Investment	Example	Comments	Upside	Probability of Return
Infra-structure	Wide area network	Support current business (may allow for future investments)	Little itself, but allows new programs	0.2 to 1.0 (0.5)
Required (no return) managerial control	OSHA reporting system; budgets	A cost of business	Almost none	0 to 0.5 (0.2)
No other way to do the job	Computerized reservations system; Air Traffic Control	Enable new task or process; provide better customer service; provide new products	Could gain more than forecast	0.5 to 1.0 (0.75)
Direct return from IT	Merrill Lynch; Chrysler	Structured, cost/benefit, and NPV appropriate	A little, if you can build on the investment	0.7 to 1.0 (0.9)
Indirect returns	CRS in travel agencies	Potential for considerable return, but indirect benefits hard to estimate	Could be substantial future benefits	0 to 1.0 (0.5)
Competitive necessity	Bank ATMs; much EDI; electronic commerce	Need the system to compete in the business; what is the cost of not investing in technology?	Very little if you are following the industry	0 to 1.0 (0.2)
Strategic application	Baxter; Merrill Lynch CMA	High risk–high potential; may be able to estimate return only after implementation	A high potential	0 to 1.0 (0.5)
Transforma-tional IT	Virtual organizations; Oticon	Must be combined with changes in management philosophy; good for fast response organization (risky to change structure, but high potential rewards)	A high potential	0 to 1.0 (0.5)

Transportation infrastructure lets the economy function by moving goods from where they are produced to where they are consumed. In eastern Europe, there have been tales of farm products rotting in the fields because there is a limited transportation infrastructure to move food to the consumer.

Technology today requires an underlying infrastructure. Experts differ as to what belongs in infrastructure. Most of us would include computers, communications networks, and some general-purpose software like database management systems. Given the rapid advance of technology, we would expect an organization to have a large number of desktop workstations (NationsBank has more computers than employees according to its chairman)—computers that are dedicated as file servers, computers that process transactions, and networks that link computers in the organization together. There should also be connections to the Internet. Increasingly, things like a home page on the Web and corporate information posted to Web pages constitute a minimal infrastructure. Groupware like Lotus Notes might also be considered a part of infrastructure.

What do you gain from investments in infrastructure? For many firms, information technology is vital to running the business. Banks, brokerage firms, and others that deal in services and transactions have long used technology as part of their production effort. Universities have a tremendous investment in infrastructure to provide technology for students and faculty. Infrastructure, then, is almost a requirement for many organizations to be in business today.

On the upside, infrastructure may also enable you to take advantage of some opportunity. The firm that develops the capability to set up a Web page and post information to it is in a good position to create an Intranet within the company. It is also better prepared for electronic commerce, since it already has a presence on the Web. It can be argued that infrastructure investment is done as much for the opportunities it opens up as for the immediate needs for which it is justified.

My own estimate is that there is about a 50 percent chance of getting a payoff that you can measure from infrastructure investments. However, like highways, railroads, and the air travel system, these kinds of investments are crucial to enabling you to do business. You may choose to do more than the minimum investment here, but that decision will be justified more on faith than on hard numbers.

Required. How can a system be required? One source of many requirements is the government. Companies have developed applications to satisfy federal or state requirements, particularly for organizations like the Occupational Safety and Health Administration (OSHA). It is hard to see a return on this kind of investment, except possibly *cost avoidance,* since there may be a fine associated with noncompliance.

When the automakers first began to insist their suppliers be able to accept orders electronically, there was little choice for vendors if they wanted to do business in the auto industry. If you demanded an economic justification, you could determine the value of sales to the auto companies and compare that with the cost of EDI. However, most managers would probably not consider non-compliance unless they sold very little to auto manufacturers. *Investing in this technology was a cost of doing business.*

Other kinds of required systems include managerial control, applications like budgeting and accounting. IT used for these purposes is important in running the company, but it is very hard to find a great deal of value, either cost savings or revenue generation, from investing in managerial control technology.

If you insist on economic justification, then the relevant numbers are likely to be opportunity costs. The question becomes, what is the cost of not making the investment, rather than what do we save or gain from this application? The upside here is almost none, since you will probably invest in this technology and move on.

No Other Way. We have mentioned computerized reservations systems, but there are many more applications of technology that would not be feasible manually. Once you are on the plane, the Air Traffic Control (ATC) system takes over. Unfortunately, while we all depend on this system, severe management and underinvestment problems have allowed the ATC system to become seriously outdated. Even with obsolete equipment, it is hard to imagine a manual replacement for it.

Think of the stock exchanges where hundreds of millions of shares trade hands every day. In the 1960s, the New York Stock Exchange had to close one day a week to clear trades with a volume that is a fraction of today's. In October 1997, the NYSE traded 1.2 billion shares in a single day. If you look at a plot of the amount of business done by commercial banks versus the number of employees, you will find that there has been a substantial growth in business with a reduction in employment. Information technology makes it possible to handle this kind of volume.

Many commercial vessels and pleasure craft use computers that display a nautical chart. A GPS (global positioning system) receiver uses a series of satellites to compute the vessel's position; it sends a signal to the computer to plot the position on the chart. Theoretically a navigator could make similar plots, but certainly not in the few seconds the system requires, and probably not with its 100-meter accuracy. Trucking companies use this technology to track their fleets, and there are consumer products appearing in automobiles that plot routes and allow a service center to determine where a car in trouble is located.

The New York-New Jersey area has been implementing electronic toll collection at bridges and tunnels; it is to be extended to toll roads as well. Eventually, the same system should be in place on much of the East Coast. We know the manual, non-IT option; it is in place today with human toll-takers and collection booths that do little to speed traffic flow. Getting motorists through the toll plazas faster would reduce their travel times and increase the capacity and utilization of the bridge, tunnel, or roadway.

The new system in the New York-New Jersey area, called EZ Pass, requires the motorist to attach a transponder to the windshield. When a car so equipped approaches a toll gate, a device at the gate reads the account number from the transponder, charges the toll, and gives the motorist a green light to proceed. A driver may have an automatic account in which his or her credit card is charged when the toll balance reaches $10, or a manual account in which one sends a check. In the case of the latter account, a sign lights at the toll plaza when it is time to add funds. Drivers receive an itemized monthly statement showing the date, time, and facility for which they were charged a toll. The manual system of toll takers has reached capacity; it is very difficult to add more toll booths in most locations. The only feasible way to expand capacity is through an investment in information technology.

If the task for which you are investing has to be done, and there is no other way but with information technology, then you probably have little choice in the matter. Some of the high-profile applications have produced substantial benefits for the companies who innovated with technology. There is considerable upside potential if you are the first organization to develop this innovation. Certainly if you are the first mover, then there is a high probability of obtaining a return from investments here; a typical number might be a 75 percent probability of obtaining returns.

A Direct Return. Applications of IT in this category are the textbook case. You can measure an expected return, evaluate the costs, and use a number of capital budgeting techniques to decide whether or not to invest. We will see examples in later chapters of an investment in new technology at Merrill Lynch for processing physical securities. We will also look at electronic data interchange and just-in-time production at Chrysler. These applications are well structured, and estimating costs and benefits are relatively easy compared to other categories in the matrix. There is a very high probability of obtaining a return from investments in systems where you see a direct benefit from the start. However, because you have identified the returns to start with, the upside potential here is probably not too great unless you can build on the system with some new innovation.

An exception to these observations on the upside comes when there is the potential to affect a large portion of an industry. We will see an example of electronic document interchange in the automobile industry; this technology has also had a major impact on grocery and clothing retailers. Health care is another field in which there is great opportunity for major cost savings (*Wall Street Journal*, June 10, 1998). It has been estimated that health-care providers spend $83 billion annually on products like latex gloves, surgical kits, and other supplies. Advocates of bar coding and scanning these supplies think they can save $11 billion a year with technology. These savings are attractive because they do not require giving up or substituting products, nor do they affect the quality of care. One leading hospital in North Dakota reduced inventory costs 48 percent, or $2.2 million, by applying bar coding to improve control.

Indirect Returns. This is a relatively new category that we have identified in some recent research on airline computerized reservations systems in travel agencies. We shall discuss these types of returns in Chapter 5. A simple example may help. Federal Express has a site on the Web where you can check on the location of packages. Before this service, the only way to check was to call a toll-free number and speak with an operator. Federal Express expects direct returns from this system through reductions in the use of its toll-free number and the ability to handle more inquiries with the same or smaller staff. *Indirect benefits* accrue from this technology if customers develop more loyalty to FedEx because it is easy to check on their package using the Internet. In a discussion of this example, a student also mentioned that she had been on hold for 30 minutes the last time she called, so the time the system saves the customer is an added indirect benefit.

This example shows how difficult it can be to measure indirect benefits. In the airline computerized reservations system (CRS) case, it was years after the development of these systems before the airlines placed terminals in travel agencies. For FedEx, how do you measure increased customer satisfaction and loyalty and relate it to revenues and profits? The potential upside is great from investments in this category, but very few applications result in significant indirect benefits. Given the difficulty of identifying indirect returns, and even of thinking what they might be, you probably are looking at a 50 percent probability or lower of obtaining indirect benefits from an investment in technology.

Competitive Necessity. While sometimes ideas for new technology innovations do not obtain an enthusiastic response from senior management, one argument that attracts notice is to say that "our competitors are developing a similar application," or worse, "our competitors have already implemented this system and are capturing market share."

One of the best examples of technology that is a competitive necessity is the bank automatic teller machine, or ATM. Several researchers have studied ATMs to see if banks have reduced costs or increased revenues at the expense of competitors. One of these investigators concluded that ATMs are simply a competitive necessity (Clemons 1990). You might find a slight advantage to the first bank that developed them, but all of that advantage has disappeared with banks forming networks of ATMs to meet customer demand for widespread ease of access. It is hard to imagine a bank today that does not offer ATMs.

At least at the time ATMs were first installed, there seemed to be few direct benefits. However, as technology matures, it is possible that an investment in this technology will have a payoff. The chairman of NationsBank mentioned earlier in this chapter indicated that the bank had closed about 150 branches in 1996 while installing between 600 and 1,000 new ATMs. If customers are ready to accept fewer branch locations, ATM technology, which first was a competitive necessity, may become a way to substantially reduce costs.

Later we shall talk about a floral company named Calyx and Corolla. This company built itself through alliances with growers and Federal Express. The headquarters of Calyx and Corolla develops plans for arrangements, prints over 12 million catalogs a year and distributes them, and takes orders for flowers. This innovative company grew to $20 million in sales within a few years of its founding. It has been used as an example of a virtual "snap together" organization.

It is interesting to note that a company which uses technology heavily in its operations (for processing orders, communicating with growers, and tracking shipments) had no presence on the Web until the spring of 1997. However, its main competitors, FTD and 1-800-FLOWERS, both had Web sites from which one could place an order. At this point, such a site is a competitive necessity for Calyx and Corolla, and it now has one.

The upside in investments in this category is probably little if you are following others in the industry. Unless you can come up with a new innovation, you are simply replicating what your competitors have. Any advantage you might gain from the system has already been competed away; my estimate is a 20 percent chance of obtaining a return from your investment in systems that are a competitive necessity.

Strategic Application. Beginning in the 1980s there was a great deal written about the strategic use of IT. American Hospital Supply, which merged with Baxter International, only to be spun off again as Allegiance, provides a 30-year history of integrating technology with strategy. Since the publicity about Baxter and a few other companies, the search for strategic applications has become very popular. Several companies like Baxter, Merrill Lynch with its cash management account, and Braun Passot, an office supply company in France, have all provided success stories. Unfortunately, these stories have very little evidence; one has to make a lot of assumptions about the impact of the technology to be convinced that IT is responsible for the firms' successes.

A few of the strategic applications became strategic only after someone recognized that a rather ordinary system could be used for another purpose. For both Baxter and Braun Passot, technology made it easier for customers to place orders with the company. Each firm took advantage of this ability to provide better service and get closer to customers by devising new strategies based on technology. It is unlikely that they recognized their order processing systems as strategic applications when they were first implemented.

In cases where the strategic nature of a system becomes obvious only after it has been installed, it will be difficult to include strategic considerations in justifying the investment. Strategic advantage is often stated in terms of increased market share, something very hard to predict because of the response of both the market and of competitors. If you can identify a system as strategic in advance, my estimate is that you have a 50 percent chance to see the kind of returns in market share you hope to obtain from your investment.

Transformational IT. This type of investment is my favorite, and of course, it is very difficult to implement. Here you use a combination of management and technology to change the basic structure of the organization. This kind of change, as we shall see in Chapter 8, requires more than technology; management has to adopt a new philosophy as well. In the examples we shall see in Chapter 8, the technology will turn out not to be all that sophisticated. However, management will use it in creative ways to define new organization structures and modes of operation.

Examples of companies in this category include those I have called "T-Form" ("T" for technology) organizations; others have described them as virtual organizations and networked companies. While the technology here is often simple, the entire change program is risky. I estimate a 50 percent chance of obtaining a return from investing in technology for the purpose of transforming the organization. This estimate is low because firms introduce many applications without obtaining the changes they expect. Often the failure to obtain organizational changes occurs because management expects the technology to be enough to change behavior. If you are looking for a major change in the organization, then it requires a significant management effort to create a transformation.

Are the Investment Types Independent?

The categories in the IT Investment Opportunities Matrix are based on research and personal experience. The previous discussion suggests that the different types of investments are independent and that a proposed IT innovation fits into only one category. It is quite possible that an IT investment will fit more than one category. Airlines developed the original computerized reservations system because these systems were thought to be the only way to handle the reservations process with the advent of jet planes. Later these systems became strategic, and demonstrated indirect returns. If you can identify multiple categories into which a proposed investment fits, then it should increase the probability that the organization obtains a return from that investment. The manager then estimates the probability of a return given, for example, that a proposed investment shows the potential for both direct and indirect benefits.

A more likely scenario is that a long-lived application of technology moves from one investment type to another as it matures and as the organization faces the decision to make additional investments in the application. It would have been very difficult for airline managers to foresee the development of airline CRS in the late 1950s when they made their first investments in this technology. In the 1970s when American and United made an investment to deploy terminals to travel agents, managers could make an argument for a direct return based on bookings fees. Did these managers also anticipate indirect benefits?

Some Evidence for the Matrix

As a part of a recent study, Ajit Kambil of New York University and I read two years' worth of letters from chairpersons in 100 annual reports looking for mentions of information technology.

Table 1-2 describes some of the applications the chairmen described which fit the different categories presented in the IT Investment Opportunities Matrix.

Allmerica is concentrating on systems that provide a direct return in the form of cost savings. Bank America focuses on its transactions processing efficiency, an application that fits into the "no other way" category. In their 1995 report, Bank America announced a Web presence, which I would categorize as both competitive and strategic, with some possible indirect benefits. Their electronic branch on America Online is an attempt to establish a first, or at least early mover, competitive advantage. Will the bank get an immediate dollar return from these electronic network investments? A return, in the short run, is probably unlikely; the bank may be buying an option here to be positioned for future applications when the opportunity arises.

Corestates Financial views its IT investment as a competitive tool. Their third-party processing business should show a direct return because they can charge fees that generate a profit. The Workplace 21 project "empowers employees to make decisions on behalf of customers"; this sounds like a project that might have indirect returns by creating more customer loyalty.

Fleet Financial wants to invest in technology to help customers "access, move, and manage their money." This investment might fit into the strategic or competitive category. Revco Drug Stores is investing in IT for efficiency and probably to reduce order cycle times. The manager's workstation is intended to create more efficiencies at the store, so Revco expects a direct return from its investments. In 1995 Revco invested $140 million to upgrade technology and improve certain systems, and it appears that a significant portion of this investment went for infrastructure. The drug store is positioning itself to be more efficient in a difficult, competitive industry.

Rohm and Haas is looking for a direct return from its investment in IT, as much as $75 million a year, which is a substantial savings.

These letters describe a variety of investments in technology that illustrate some of the different types found in Table 1-1. The majority of the initiatives fall into the "direct return" category, as shareholders like to hear about reduced expenses and increased revenues. The chairpersons also see some of these IT efforts leading to a competitive advantage, at least in the Revco case, allowing

Table 1-2

Excerpts from Corporate Annual Reports Regarding IT Investments

---

"Communication with agencies regarding policy information has improved substantially through greater use of on-line agency management systems, which downloads policy information directly to agency offices... Our challenge is to balance investments in technology with expense management, an area of focus for 1995... We expect to begin to realize cost savings from our investments in technology and process reengineering programs, and to see the overall expense ratio beginning to improve in 1995." (Allmerica Property & Casualty Cos., Inc., 1994)

"We will continue to seek further operating economics, and to advance technology solutions wherever feasible. For example, we will invest in Corporate Risk Management Services business as it continues to pursue growth opportunities in nontraditional markets, but we will also leverage this unit's expertise to manage health care costs better." (Allmerica, 1995)

"We are highly competent at large-scale, efficient high-volume processing to support customer transactions. We clear approximately 20 million checks nightly—nearly ten percent of the national total—cost-effectively. Cumulatively, we are the largest bank processor of ATM, credit and debit card and automated clearing house transactions in the western United States. Altogether, approximately 40 percent of the GDP in the West is processed through Bank America.... In retail banking we continued... opening experimental self-service branches, expanding our in-store branch network, and creating a Bank America presence on the Internet." (Bank America, 1994)

"We have established an interactive presence on the Internet's World Wide Web and opened an electronic branch on America Online." (Bank America, 1995)

"During 1995 we affirmed in many ways our belief in technology as an important competitive tool. We invested in improved technology for consumer and business banking services and also in our third party processing businesses. We initiated a project, Workplace 21, to develop the internal information supports for further progress in empowering employees to make decisions on behalf of customers. Late in the year we launched a broad strategic review of future technology needs." (Corestates Financial, 1995)

"A second and related byproduct of Fleet Focus was the realization that we had to make a much heavier capital commitment to technology. Perhaps the single greatest challenge our industry faces today is to harness technological advances to help customers access, move, and manage their money." (Fleet Financial, 1994)

---

continued on next page

Table 1-2
continued from previous page

"Our investment in technology will also continue in 1995. The development of a major system to reorder merchandise for the stores and distribution centers, and a manager's workstation to facilitate more efficiencies at the store level, are high priority projects." (Revco DS, 1994)

"Revco invested approximately $140 million this past year to upgrade technology and improve the condition of our store base and distributor systems... Also Revco must invest in technology to improve productivity, and leverage costs against pressured prescription margins, to respond effectively in a consolidating industry." (Revco DS, 1995)

"We are building a single, integrated computer network that accepts orders, assigns inventory, forecasts future requirements, schedules plant production, replenishes stocks and keeps track of costs. This system allows a person sitting in our French office to take a phone call from a U.K. customer and—while the customer is still on the phone—arrange for product to be shipped from a plant or warehouse anywhere in Europe... . We began to see cost savings from this system in 1994 and expect even greater savings over the next few years—perhaps as much as $75 million per year by the end of the decade." (Rohm and Haas, 1994)

---

the firm to compete in a changing industry. This sampler shows that managers have a variety of reasons for undertaking many different types of IT initiatives.

A Personal View

Figure 1-1 presents my conclusions about investments in information technology. Much of the rest of this book is devoted to providing evidence of returns from investing in IT, and to suggestions of where a return is unlikely or virtually impossible to measure.

Organizations invest in the categories of application delineated in the Investment Opportunities Matrix and shown on the left side of Figure 1-1. The organization tries to convert each investment into a working application of IT. When implemented, that investment may create direct savings or generate additional revenue for the firm. There may be indirect returns and a major organizational change from the investment. Unfortunately, there can also be partial successes and outright failures. The second-order impact of this investment may accrue to the consumer through better products and services. The

Figure 1-1

The Payoff from Investments in IT

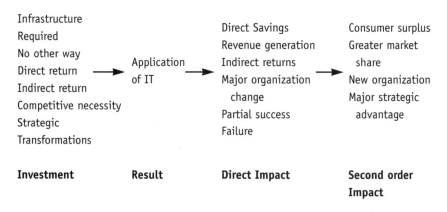

Infrastructure Required		Direct Savings	Consumer surplus
No other way		Revenue generation	Greater market
Direct return	Application	Indirect returns	share
Indirect return	of IT	Major organization	New organization
Competitive necessity		change	Major strategic
Strategic		Partial success	advantage
Transformations		Failure	
Investment	**Result**	**Direct Impact**	**Second order Impact**

investing firm may gain market share or a major strategic advantage. It may create an entirely new organizational form enabled by IT.

Successful investors spread their funds over a portfolio of applications from the Investment Opportunities Matrix. These firms spend on infrastructure so they are ready when an opportunity comes along. Some applications in their portfolio will probably fail, and others may be a partial success. However, certain applications provide a major contribution to the firm, the way shares of Microsoft purchased ten years ago enhance a stock portfolio.

I believe, after reviewing the evidence, that the total impact of investments in technology is more than the sum of their individual contributions. Applications of IT interact with one another, creating new benefits and opportunities. For example, a brokerage company is an early innovator with a Web site; it uses this experience to build an Intranet for all of its research output. Suddenly, all research in the firm is available to any professional, and the firm has dramatically reduced its publication costs. Management turns the Intranet into an Extranet by allowing key customers to have access to it; through this vehicle the company provides its research to customers and establishes a closer relationship with them. The firm gradually finds its structure changing as more employees have direct links to clients; there is less need for a hierarchy of management and for support staff. Applications of technology enhance one another and become woven into the fabric of the organization. It may even be difficult to identify specific applications as technological innovation becomes a part of doing business. Therefore, it seems that *the cumulative impact of investments in information technology exceed the sum of their individual contributions.*

A Preview

This chapter has set the stage for what is to come. I have tried to make the point that one cannot expect returns from every investment in information technology. Even if you do expect such returns, it is not 100 percent certain that you will be able to attain them. Thinking carefully about what kind of application you are undertaking should help place the probabilities in perspective.

The next chapter illustrates graphically why it can be difficult to realize returns from IT investments, building on the Opportunities Matrix. We will introduce another confounding factor in obtaining a return, the probability that the development of the technology is successful. We will motivate and introduce two important concepts, the *IT Investment Equation* and the *IT Value Equation*. These two equations make a fundamental contribution to understanding the expected value from investments in IT. The rest of this book will present examples of systems where there appears to be considerable evidence that the company deploying the technology did obtain a return from its investment. My objective is to show that *it is possible to obtain value from investing in technology, even though every investment may not show a measurable return.*

Part II of the book tries to make the case that value has come from specific investments in information technology. In this part, we look at the evidence from groups of firms and from individual organizations where direct returns occurred. In Part III we review the categories of indirect returns and infrastructure investments. We also explore technology as a part of strategy and for changing organizations. Part IV looks at ways to increase the chances for successful investment, and Part V offers implications for managing information technology and for where to find IT value.

While I have argued that not every application of technology will necessarily demonstrate value, I believe that IT offers tremendous advantages to organizations, the economy, and society. In a market economy, we use investment criteria to determine where to allocate resources most efficiently. In order to make this allocation, we have to understand where to expect returns from investing in IT, and how to estimate and evaluate these returns. A search for value from information technology should help in making decisions about IT investments.

CHAPTER TWO

A Garbage Can Model and the
IT Investment/Value Equations

In the first chapter we saw that there are many different kinds of applications of information technology. Understanding that each of these different types has different potential for a return is the first step in searching for IT value. This chapter focuses on the second step, the ability to obtain the expected returns from an IT initiative.

When a company buys an asset like a new truck to make deliveries, it can estimate reasonably well the operating costs for the new vehicle and compare them with the costs of its old truck. If the new truck has more capacity, the firm can calculate the increased revenue from being able to carry more goods and compare that with its operating costs. For the most part, the buyer of the truck can be assured that the truck will operate, that is, it will carry a certain payload at a reasonable speed, meeting its operating specifications. There is little uncertainty associated with the cost or payback from the investment in the truck.

Are circumstances similar with an investment in technology? The answer to this question is a resounding "no," and in this chapter we explore why this is so. The chapter introduces another probability into the calculation of the return from investing in information technology, completing our explanation of why one does not always get what is expected from IT initiatives.

Garbage Can Models

Are organizations the carefully structured inventions we see on organization charts? In 1972 some noted researchers offered an alternative to the traditional picture of the organization; they named their theory the "garbage can model" (Cohen, March, and Olsen 1972). These researchers describe organizations as organized anarchies.

Their anarchies have three main properties. First, organizations operate on a series of inconsistent and ill-defined preferences. There is more of a loose collection of ideas than a coherent structure. To discover preferences, an observer has to look at actions because the preferences that managers express are not the preferences they actually use.

Second, members of the organization do not really understand its processes. The kind of learning that occurs is trial and error; we learn from the accidents of past experience. This uncertainty about what is happening is particularly true for technology.

The third characteristic of organized anarchies is the capricious action of its members. People in organizations vary in the amount of time and effort they devote to different activities. This inconsistency creates uncertain boundaries for the organization, and changes the audience of participants in different decision situations.

According to Cohen, March, and Olsen (1972), "An organization is a collection of choices looking for problems, issues in which they might be aired, solutions looking for issues to which they might be the answer, and decision makers looking for work." The picture is of a giant garbage can with issues, choices, problems, solutions, and decision makers all floating around together. There are four streams flowing through the can: a stream of choices, one of problems, a flow of solutions, and a stream of energy from decision makers.

Does anyone believe the garbage can model? Is it a tongue-in-cheek critique of organizations and, in particular, experts who describe them as purposeful, decision-making entities? Different models provide perspective on a problem by encouraging us to think in different ways about it; the garbage can model is one of these. If companies are structured, problem-solving entities, why do they sometimes miss a problem with disastrous results? Why did IBM cling to the mainframe model for so long, and then need to reduce its number of employees by 50 percent? Is this period in the company's history best explained by rational decision-making, or by a garbage can model where decision makers ignored a problem or did not recognize it as a threat?

Garbage Cans and IT Investment

Investments in information technology are replete with uncertainty. We are dealing with a great deal of complexity, with the need to fit unknown technology to processes in an organization that can be abstract and hard to understand. I think a garbage can model of IT value portrays the situation most organizations confront when making investments in technology. This model is depicted in Figure 2-1.

Floating around in the garbage can are the actors and the technology that combine to produce IT initiatives. A key group in implementing an IT initiative is the IT staff, the individuals who specialize in creating and deploying technology. Members of the IT staff include analysts, programmers, project managers, network and communications specialists, operations personnel, and individuals who offer help to users. In a typical IT initiative, we also find users. These people come from any level of the organization, and it is unfortunate that senior managers often delegate the user role to low levels in the firm.

There often are consultants involved in developing new information technology, partially because of the complexity of the technology and the large number of choices available. A good example of the consultant's role is with the integrated package called R/3 from SAP. The entire suite of applications in R/3 provides a comprehensive set of functions for managing a business, from financial statements to production control. A large number of firms have adopted this package (SAP claims 12,000 customers), including Colgate Palmolive, IBM, Compaq, Chevron, and Lucent Technologies. R/3's success has created a whole new consulting industry; most of the Big Six accounting firms have large SAP practices. In fact, this package is so dependent on outside expertise for implementation that its sales may be constrained by lack of consulting capacity in the industry! (It has been estimated that there are over 3,000 decisions to be made in configuring R/3; the product has some 8,000 configuration tables!)

Senior management is also involved in a technology initiative, at least in theory. One expects senior managers to be responsible for what goes on in the organization. In general, the more this group gets involved in IT decisions and implementations, the better the results.

All of these actors work with both tangibles and intangibles that float by. The tangibles are easy to understand; they include the IT infrastructure of computers, networks, databases, and software. This technology is complex, and all parts must work together. Whether you buy a software package or write programs from scratch, software must run on the hardware that you buy or already have installed. Computers execute millions of instructions per second; requests for service come in at random intervals, and it can be difficult or impossible to re-create the exact scenario that resulted in a system failure. Computer scientists have proven that no program is ever fully debugged. Making the technology work is an extremely challenging task!

Figure 2–1
A Garbage Can Model of IT Value

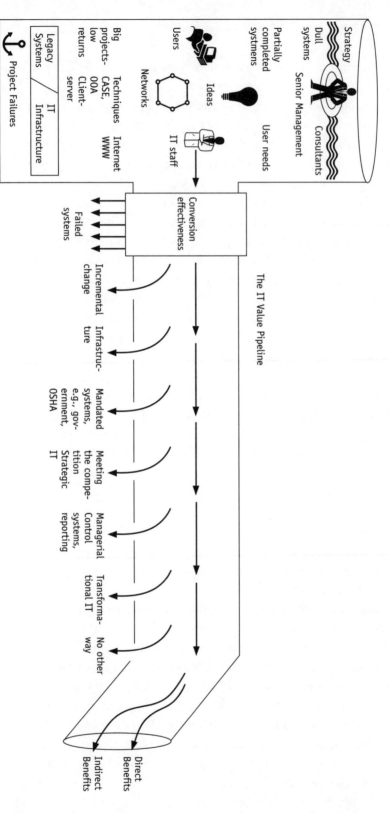

The intangibles that confront everyone working on an IT investment are user and organization needs, ideas, and strategy. One of the crucial stages in developing any system is requirements analysis, that is, trying to figure out what users want the system to do. It is much more difficult than you think for people to explain their needs for technology; the task gets even harder when you are trying to undertake a major redesign of the way work is done. It is very common to have individuals who are in similar functions describe needs and potential systems that are totally different from each other.

Ideas are what drive progress; some of the most creative and successful systems originated with user ideas. For many years, American Hospital Supply and then Baxter (after a takeover) ran its strategic order entry application with a separate IT operation in marketing, rather than through the traditional IS function. In the 1960s, a sales representative had the idea for connecting a customer directly with the system. The company built on that idea to integrate technology with its products, selling value-added services in addition to hospital products. Users and managers suggest many of the innovative applications of technology on the Internet and the World Wide Web. Ideas from a variety of sources are critical to finding innovative IT investments.

The last intangible is corporate strategy. I once worked with a company chairman who kept the company's strategy to himself for fear that it would fall into the hands of the competition. I would argue that it is not knowledge of your strategy that determines success, it is how well you execute the strategy. By keeping employees in the dark, it was hard for them to come up with ideas that helped the company follow its strategy. In the culture of openness one finds on the Web, some companies even publish their strategy on their home pages!

The garbage can model can help us understand why not all IT investments are successful. Before we apply this model, the chapter presents evidence to support the contention that IT projects have in the past not met expectations or have failed outright.

Project Success and Other Outcomes

We began the chapter with an example of a company buying a new truck. It would be hard to imagine that the investment in the truck would fail, that is, you would buy the truck and find that it could not carry the goods you planned to ship, or worse yet, that you could not drive the truck because it would not start, you could not steer it, or some other mechanical failure made it inoperative. Can we say the same about systems?

- PG&E, the largest publicly owned electric and gas utility, canceled a $100 million customer information system reengineering project. IBM's Global Services integration group had a contract for this project. PG&E said that the package solution it was attempting to implement could not keep up with the "lightning-fast changes in the services industry." Thousands of support representatives use this system to help 13 million customers. The existing system was too inflexible to meet new rate structures and the challenges of deregulation. One problem was defining the scope of the new system; another was that the date for deregulation moved up (*PC Week,* April 28, 1997).

- In 1997, the U.S. General Accounting Office criticized the IRS's modernization project saying that the agency would have to scrap the project and start over. The IRS has canceled one project to turn paper tax returns into electronic images after paying a contractor $284 million for it. The IRS is reviewing some 12 projects to see if they should be terminated. In total, the IRS admits that it has spent $4 billion developing modern computer systems that a top official said "do not work in the real world." Today, customer service representatives (the IRS considers us to be its "customers") must use as many as nine terminals, each connected to different databases, to research problems (*New York Times,* January 31, 1997).

- The automated baggage handling system at the new Denver airport was blamed for expensive delays in opening the airport, some three times in seven months. The contractor, BAE, had a $175.6 million contract to build one of the most sophisticated baggage handling systems yet developed for the entire Denver airport. As might be expected, when delays occurred, there was much finger-pointing between the airport and the baggage contractor. Upon opening, the fully automated system was working for United, the largest tenant, while more conventional systems existed elsewhere (Montealegre and Nelson, 1996).

- The joint effort between American Airlines, SABRE Technologies, and Mariott Hotels to develop a major travel supermarket system was canceled among a flurry of lawsuits. The initial estimates for the cost of the project were $55.7 million; it was canceled due to significant management failures after 3.5 years and $125 million in costs (Ewusi-Mensah, 1997).

- The secretary of transportation canceled a long-running, expensive air traffic control modernization project after the government spent billions of dollars on the project. Some experts suggest that IBM sold its Federal Systems Division, the prime contractor for the FAA, to isolate itself from this project. The design had a number of flaws, including a lengthy development time that rendered it obsolete. The original concept was for the ground controllers to inform pilots of their location as determined by ground radar. The satellite-based global positioning system became widely available during the system design, and it can provide a more accurate location for the pilot than the controller from the ground. Providing the information directly in the cockpit reduces communications requirements and the processing load on the human controller.

- Dell Computer recently halted an extensive SAP R/3 implementation (*ComputerWorld,* May 26, 1997). In its place the PC vendor is developing its own architecture, including a large number of proprietary and packaged software modules, including SAP's human resources management software. A spokesperson for the company said that, given its explosive growth, trying to implement tightly integrated applications with three different consulting groups did not make a lot of sense. Some of the SAP licenses that Dell purchased will end up going unused.

Unfortunately there are many more such stories. However, as we shall see in the rest of the book, there are many examples of successful IT investments as well. What is the overall picture? How successful have organizations been in implementing their IT investments? A consulting firm has estimated, based on a survey of 360 companies, that in 1996, 73 percent of U.S. software projects were canceled, over budget, or late, down from 84 percent the previous year. The good news is that less than 20 percent fall into the canceled category; the majority of the 73 percent are simply late or over budget. The Standish Group estimates that IS project failures cost $45 billion in 1996 (*ComputerWorld,* February 24, 1997).

Definitions and classification are tricky here. First, we are dealing with large, multiuser projects. Users routinely develop thousands of spreadsheets, small databases, and applications in systems like Lotus Notes that are highly successful. However, most of these projects, in my experience, involve users working on their own without a formal project and budget. We can consider their efforts the results of an earlier investment in IT infrastructure that provides a workstation, software, and a network.

It would be helpful to have statistics on how late projects are on average, and how much they are over budget. A late project delays the benefits that you are expecting from your investment. In the worst case, the project is too late to meet a competitive challenge or a deadline and ends up being canceled like the PG&E system above. An over-budget project reduces the return that you expected when deciding to make an investment in information technology. A small overrun is probably not a problem, but anything significant could dramatically alter the expected return on investment (ROI).

Is "late and over budget" unique to technology investments? I suspect not. The Denver airport was late and over budget before any problem with the baggage system surfaced. One frequently reads about new product launches that are late and over budget; Detroit, and in particular GM, has had significant problems introducing and producing new models on time and in budget. One reason for problems with nuclear power is the consistent pattern of cost and time overruns in building plants. Information technology is not unique; forecasting the tasks required, their sequence, and possible problems for complex jobs like constructing a new airport, a new automobile, or an innovation using information technology is very difficult. While not excusing cost and time overruns, the prudent manager should factor their likelihood into any return on investment calculations.

The Concept of Conversion Effectiveness

The garbage can model for IT value in Figure 2-1 sends various projects down the pipe toward a "return on investment" spigot. The first thing they encounter is a filter called "conversion effectiveness," a concept suggested by Weill (1990). This filter is defined "as the effectiveness with which investments in IT are converted into useful outputs." Weill measured four components of conversion effectiveness, including top management commitment, experience with IT, user satisfaction, and turbulence of the firm's political environment.

Although these components undoubtedly influence the conversion of the IT investment into a successful project, there are many more factors that influence success. My list includes the following, and you can probably add some that I have overlooked:

Size and scope of the project

Amount of unknown technology involved

Project management

Support and encouragement of managers, sponsorship

The urgency of the problem/opportunity addressed by the technology

Norms in the organization

User commitment and involvement

Technical development environment

Quality of the IT staff

Strength of the project team

Level of expertise of participants

Type of technology employed

Type of application

Amount of custom code written

Nature of packaged software included

Use of external consultants

Degree of understanding between users and developers

Presence of a project champion

Senior management involvement

Amount of organizational change required

Threat to existing personnel, vested interests

User's views of the quality of the system

There are many variables that partially determine conversion effectiveness. A failure on any one of the items listed above can doom a project, *even if every other aspect of development is successful.*

Estimates for the probability of successful conversion are the responsibility of IT staff members, consultants, outsourcing staff members, and other professionals with experience in the field. These individuals, given the nature of a proposed IT investment, should be able to estimate the probability of conversion success. They will base this estimate on their own past experience, the kind of technology the project requires, the capabilities of those working on the project, and other factors such as those listed earlier.

The Information Technology Investment Equation

We now have two influences on the return one can expect from investing in information technology. The first, from Chapter 1, is the Investment Opportunities Matrix shown in Table 1-1. The right-most column of this table suggests that each opportunity does not necessarily have a probability of 1 for a return from an investment in IT. For the Chrysler EDI/JIT system to be discussed later, the probability of a return was quite high. For a budgeting system or a government report, the probability is low.

In Chapter 1, we implicitly assumed that an investment in IT would be successful, something that companies seem to do regularly. I do not recall ever seeing a justification for a system that suggested the project might not meet 100 percent of its objectives on time and within budget! Following this common practice, we estimated the probabilities in Table 1-1 assuming successful conversion. We also assumed the estimates of a return, given a particular investment type, are independent of other events.

In this chapter we have seen that the ability of the organization to implement technology introduces a probability of success once you make a decision to invest. To calculate the probability of obtaining a return on an IT investment, we need to weight the probability that an investment type will show a return by the probability of successful conversion.

Before we look at an example or any equations, I would like to appeal to intuition. If there is a chance that a type of IT investment will not have the full return forecast, we should expect less of a return than those who proposed the project suggested. If a project team forecasts a return of $100,000 and we think there is less than a 100 percent chance of getting that return, then we expect to see less than the $100,000. The amount will be reduced because we do not expect this type of investment to provide a full return. Perhaps the project with the forecasted $100,000 return drops to an estimated return of $80,000 given the type of project.

In this chapter, we introduced the idea of conversion effectiveness. If we are not completely successful in converting an IT investment into a working application, then we would expect to further reduce the returns from the investment. Then, the estimated return of $80,000 drops again because we are not sure of being completely successful in converting the IT investment into a successful application. This failure to achieve 100 percent conversion success might drop our estimated return to, say, $65,000.

Even if you do not agree with the numbers, or are not fond of the more formal treatment that follows, I hope your intuition agrees that the estimated returns from a project will often be less than the original forecast. This reduction in estimated return is due to the contention in Chapter 1 that some types of IT investment are unlikely to show a full return, and the discussion in this chapter about conversion effectiveness and a historical lack of total success in developing IT applications. Later in this chapter we give some examples and present two equations that are important in Chapter 10 when we discuss possible ways to make decisions about IT investments.

We look at a simple example now, adding probabilities. Suppose that you are reviewing a proposed IT project to let customers track their orders over the Internet. Because several of your competitors already offer this feature, it is proposed as a competitive necessity. A task force studying this project estimates that you will save $500,000 a year on customer service expenses because some customers will be able to answer their own inquiries. They also feel that their design is superior to that of the competition, and you will gain $250,000 in additional profits from increased market share. Examining the proposal, you estimate that there is a 0.5 probability that you will get the return suggested by the task force because (1) your design may not be that much better than the competition, (2) if all your competitors move to the Net it is unlikely you will increase market share, and (3) it is not clear that a significant percentage of your customers will use the new service.

Can you now state confidently that the project has a 0.5 probability of being successful and generating a return? The analysis mentioned previously assumes that you are 100 percent successful in developing this Internet initiative for your customers. Based on the examples in this chapter, the garbage can model, and the history of IT development in your own organization, is that likely? Given your doubts, you take the project proposal to three very experienced, very candid IT staff members and ask them to predict the probability that the company can implement the Internet initiative with all of the features in the report. These three staff members come back with estimated probabilities of successful conversion of 0.7, 0.8 and 0.9, and you take the average at 0.8.

Now we have two numbers, a 0.5 probability of a return given the type and characteristics of the proposed IT project, and a 0.8 probability that the firm can successfully convert that proposal into an application that has all of its features. We have treated the return and successful conversion as independent events. The laws of probability theory tell us that the probability of two independent events happening is found by multiplying the probability of each event alone. Thus, the probability of a return given the type of application *and* successfully converting the proposal into a system is 0.5 multiplied by 0.8, which is 0.4.

If the idea of multiplying the two probabilities together is not clear, a contrived coin toss example may clarify our approach. Assume that you have been asked to toss two quite unfair coins, a quarter and a nickel. The quarter has a 60 percent chance of coming up heads and 40 percent of tails. The nickel is even worse: it has a 70 percent chance of landing heads and a 30 percent chance of tails. The order in which you toss the coins does not matter; let's assume that you flip the quarter first and then the nickel. The possible outcomes are shown in Figure 2-2.

Figure 2–2
Tossing Two Very Unfair Coins

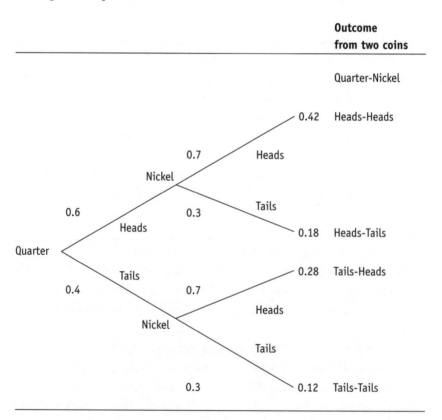

What is the probability that the two coins will both come up heads? Figure 2-2 shows that this result is the probability the quarter lands heads times the probability that the nickel lands heads, or 0.6 × 0.7 = 0.42. (Look at the top lines in the figure; they show a 0.6 probability for tossing the quarter coming up heads, at which point you toss the nickel; the top line of that toss is a 0.7 for coming up heads.) If you were to repeat the two-coin toss a large number of times, you would observe both coins landing heads about 42 percent of the time. Similarly, you can trace the probability of any of the possible combined outcomes of tossing the quarter first followed by the nickel in Figure 2–2. The reason you can multiply the probability of each event times the other is because the coin tosses are independent, that is, tossing the quarter has no influence on how the nickel lands.

We follow the same logic to get the probability of a successful return on an IT investment: Multiply the probability of a return given a particular type of IT investment times the probability of conversion success. We assume that the probability of a return on an IT initiative based on the investment type is independent of the probability of converting the investment into a successful application. You could argue that the type of investment is correlated with project size, for example, a required government report is probably a much smaller project than a strategic application. However, I do not believe such is necessarily the case. An OSHA report in the chemical industry might require a substantial system for monitoring the exposure of all workers in the company to certain chemicals. Being the first in your industry to set up a Web page to accept incoming orders might give you a first-mover advantage from relatively simple technology. I have seen projects of varying size and complexity in all of the cells of the Investments Opportunities Matrix. If a project is very large, and you think that size reduces the chances for success, then your estimate of the probability of successful conversion should reflect your concern. This line of reasoning leads to the *IT Investment Equation*:

P(Success/Return) = P(Return on Investment Type) × P(Conversion Success)

where P means "probability of." The IT Investment Equation says that the probability of obtaining a return on an investment in information technology is the probability the type of investment you are making has a return times the probability that you will be successful in converting the investment into a working IT application. The IT Investment Equation calculates a number that we will refer to in later chapters as the SR index, the probability of a successful return.

A few examples will help to illustrate what the equation means. In Table 2–1 there are four columns. The first is the type of investment. The second is an estimate by management and the IT staff of the probability that there will be a return given the nature of the investment. The third column is the probability of a successful conversion of the investment into a functioning system. According to our reasoning and the IT Investment Equation, the product of these two probabilities gives the overall probability of obtaining a return from this investment.

The table illustrates how hard it can be to obtain a return from IT investments. For a hypothetical budgeting system, management feels there is only a 50 percent chance the organization will obtain any return, since the new application replaces an old budgeting system. It has a nicer interface and better reports, but managers could not honestly say the system will help them make more money. The 50 percent figure is based on the belief that there will be some labor savings. The IT staff thinks the package will be easy to implement and estimates a 100 percent chance of successful conversion. The probability, then, of a successful return on this investment is 0.5×1.0, or 0.5.

Table 2-1
Examples of Using the IT Investment Equation

Type of Investment	Estimate of Probability of a Return Based on the Type of Project	Estimate of Probability of Successful Conversion Effort	Overall Probability of a Return: the SR Index
Budgeting system	0.5	1.0	0.5
EDI/JIT system	0.95	0.75	0.71
Infrastructure network	0.5	0.7	0.35
Package tracking system	0.2	1.0	0.2
Groupware	0.9	0.8	0.72
Web order entry	0.9	0.7	0.63
Web home pages	0	1.0	0

In the second example, management is certain that, after seeing the results at other companies, an EDI/JIT system for its factories will have a significant, measurable return. They are certain enough to estimate the probability 0.95. The IT staff, however, is a little concerned with the scope of the project, and is willing to estimate a probability of only 0.75 that it can implement the system so all the benefits occur. The probability of a successful return, then, is 0.95 × 0.75, or 0.71.

The rest of Table 2-1 illustrates other hypothetical scenarios: an infrastructure investment, an overnight delivery firm investing in a package tracking system, order entry on the World Wide Web, and Web home pages. Note the probabilities and how each one has a substantial effect on the probability of a successful return from investing in IT. *Anything less than a probability of 1 for a return on the type of investment and a probability of 1 for conversion success dramatically reduces the probability that you will be successful in obtaining a return on an IT investment.*

Estimating Returns

Almost all IT initiatives involve some estimate of costs and benefits so that those making the decision to invest have a sense of the dollars involved. Managers are in the position of having to predict the return for specific investments in technology proposed by various actors in the organization. If we look at Table 1-1 (page 12), the difficulty of making these estimates is evident.

For applications that offer a direct return, by definition estimates are not too difficult. When we look at a case of indirect returns later in the book, we shall see how difficult it is to define and measure these kinds of benefits. It has been suggested that infrastructure investments provide you with the opportunity to undertake some initiative in the future; you are buying an option to invest again. But how much is that option worth? What is its price and where is the market for it?

What is the estimated return for a system that is a competitive necessity? What is the estimated return for technology when it is the only way to do the job? Some experts suggest that you should look at the *cost of not investing*. What would happen to a new bank that failed to deploy ATMs? Could it remain in business? Would it end up being unable to build market share? If a valued customer says you must implement an EDI package, the cost is clear: losing the customer's business. Does that amount of business become the return on the investment in IT?

We must continue to attempt to estimate the return from investments in technology so that we can allocate scarce resources as effectively as possible.

However, managers should realize the imprecision and difficulty of making these estimates. The Investment Opportunities Matrix is intended to illustrate these problems.

The IT Value Equation

Managers usually do not think in terms of probabilities; they prefer dollar estimates. However, if there are probabilities involved, the decision maker should weight the dollar estimates with the probability of actually realizing the dollars. If a geologist tells an oil company executive that there is a 60 percent probability a field contains oil that is worth $100 million, what revenue should the executive *expect* to receive from the field? The executive's *expected value* is the probability the field has oil times the value of the oil, or 0.6 × $100 million, which is $60 million. In general, expected value is the amount expected times the probability that you will receive that amount.

If, in the example in Figure 2-2, you were offered $10 every time heads came up on both the quarter and the nickel, how much money would you expect to make? There are 10 throws, and each has a potential for a payoff of $10. The total at risk for the person offering the reward is 10 tosses times $10, or $100. Would you expect to win $100? Obviously not, based on Figure 2-2. You would expect heads to come up on both of these unfair coins 42 percent of the time (probability 0.42). Therefore, your expected winnings are $100 × 0.42, or $42. Here again, we are taking the amount expected times the probability that you will receive it.

In addition to estimating the probability of a return in the Investment Opportunities Matrix, most companies would try to estimate the dollar returns from investing in technology. Typically these returns are cost savings, cost avoidance, and/or new sources of revenue. If you estimate that the EDI/JIT system in Table 2-2 will save the company $1 million in its first year, then the actual expected savings will be your estimated savings times the probability of a return times the IT staff estimate of conversion success, or $1 million × 0.95 × 0.75 = $712,500. This reasoning leads to the *IT Value Equation:*

Expected Return = Estimated Return × P(Return) × P(Conversion Success) or

= Estimated Return × P(Success/Return) or

= Estimated return × IT Investment Equation

where P means probability. *The IT Value Equation shows that the expected return from an IT investment is rarely the amount estimated by those involved; it must be weighted by the probability of obtaining the return and the probability of successfully converting the investment into a working application.*

Back to the Pipeline

The conversion-effectiveness filter resulted in a lengthy digression from the garbage can model, but an important one. We now have a conceptual basis for understanding some of the problems in finding IT value. *The type of investment and the firm's success in converting the investment into a working IT application determines whether there will be a measurable financial value from investing in information technology.* The rest of the pipeline exiting the garbage can in Figure 2-1 shows some types of investment that have a good chance of falling by the wayside. At the end of the spigot are the two types of systems where you can find quantifiable value, those with a direct return and those that provide indirect benefits.

Other types of investments may or may not provide much of a return (though they may still provide other types of value). The pipeline illustrates graphically the various categories in the Investment Opportunities Matrix. Infrastructure and mandated systems like managerial control applications have a tendency to leak from the pipeline. It is hard to get investments to keep up with the competition, and many strategic applications, to the end of the line. IT that transforms a business or the entire organization has the potential for high returns, but those returns often defy measurement. Where there is no other way but technology, you may be able to identify a return by looking at infeasible alternatives, like hiring a thousand clerks to do the job.

Putting It All Together

We have discovered a number of important ideas in the first two chapters. Some key points follow:

- There are many different types of value that result from an investment in information technology. An investment may fail to provide a measurable financial return and yet still have value.

- The type of technology investment influences the probability of obtaining a return. The Investment Opportunities Matrix is intended to illustrate this insight.

- Estimating the return from an investment in technology is difficult, as shown by the examples in the Investment Opportunities Matrix.

- The garbage can model presents a graphical view of the factors that influence IT investments.

- Conversion effectiveness influences whether there will be a return from an investment. Just deciding to invest in IT does not guarantee that the investment will provide the expected return; there is a probability of success in implementing new technology.

- The IT Investment Equation says that the overall probability of return from an investment is the product of the probability that the type of investment will show a return times the probability of conversion success.

- The IT Value Equation says that management's expected value from an IT investment should be weighted by the probability calculated in the IT investment equation.

Having established the conceptual background for the book, we turn now to the task of showing that IT value exists. We will look for instances where the return on technology investments is clear and cannot be easily refuted. Then we will examine instances where estimating benefits are more difficult, and will propose ways to help solve some of the measurement problems discussed in this chapter. The idea is to show where IT value is likely to be found, and to discuss how to evaluate investments where there may be little apparent, measurable financial return using conventional measures like ROI.

PART II

IT Investments Among and Within Firms

The first place we look for value is among groups of firms. Studies of a large number of companies provide evidence at a highly aggregated level. Research within a single industry also offers insights on the nature of the return from investing in IT. A recent study of a large number of manufacturing and service firms suggests very high returns from IT investment, but the results are almost too good to believe.

One type of IT investment is expected to show a direct return; these applications are generally well structured and often involve substituting capital for labor. Our best examples for claiming a return on investment in IT are found in Chapter 4. In addition to direct returns, the chapter discusses applications where IT is the only way to do a job. Performing the same task with labor would require too many employees, create confusion in trying to organize work, and probably fail because this approach could not meet response-time requirements. For example, it would be hard to imagine trading today's volume of stocks on the world's exchanges if all trading and settlement took place manually.

CHAPTER 3

The Evidence for a Return Across
Groups of Companies

To provide convincing evidence that there is a return from investing in information technology, we have to locate some examples of value, and the strongest evidence comes from financial results. In this chapter we discuss several studies of firms in an effort to show value from IT investments. There have been a number of studies of IT investment by different groups, for example, information systems academics and economists; this chapter focuses on studies that have shown mostly positive returns. These studies provide cause for optimism, though one of them has such positive results that it is hard to believe!

It has proven very difficult to study the return from investing in information technology, particularly if you would like to relate that investment with the overall performance of a company. Consider the typical large firm with over $100 million a year in sales. What is the likelihood that anyone can track the return from a single investment in IT to the bottom line?

A graduate student planned a dissertation on such a topic a few years ago. His first proposal was to study electronic data interchange in the insurance industry and show how it contributed to firm profitability. After a few discussions, he was convinced that the bottom line of a major insurance company is determined by so many different factors it would be nearly impossible to show the impact of an investment in EDI technology.

Even if an investigator were to find that a newly deployed IT application was highly correlated with improved financial performance of the firm, in most instances it would be very difficult to claim that the technology actually caused the improved performance. In the organization studies literature, this problem is known as *causal ambiguity*. In real organizations as opposed to laboratories where a researcher conducts controlled experiments, it is very hard to control for extraneous sources of causality. For the past few years the value of stocks in the United States has risen rapidly. Investment banks and brokerage firms are experiencing record profits; what kind of evidence would you need to believe that these profits came from, or at least were partially due to, investments in information technology rather than the strong stock market?

IT in the Valve Industry

One way to provide stronger evidence than data from a single company is to look at a group of firms. The researcher gains some control by concentrating on the firms in a single industry. If this industry is relatively small and the firms in it are all about the same size, so much the better. One study was conducted under such conditions: Peter Weill looked at firms in the valve industry in his doctoral dissertation. (The study won an award as the best information system doctoral dissertation for the year and was published as a book; see Weill, 1990.) This study also played an important role in the thinking behind the Investment Opportunities Matrix discussed in Chapter 1.

The valve industry consists of small firms or divisions of larger companies. The study described here focused on strategic business units (SBUs), and a total of 33 valve manufacturers cooperated in the research. In the late 1980s, the manufacturers had an average sales of $88 million a year and employed 754 people. Some 42 percent of the participants were privately held firms, and the remainder were the autonomous subsidiaries of larger companies. The industry could be characterized by slow, steady growth.

The study was concerned with three major classes of variables:

1. Investments in different types of information technology

2. Measures of organizational performance

3. Conversion effectiveness (the ability to convert IT investments into productive applications)

Data for the study came from the CEO, controller, and production manager in each firm. They responded to questions about three categories of IT investments: strategic, informational, and transactional.

A firm undertakes strategic applications to provide a competitive advantage through increased sales and/or market share. Informational applications provide reports like sales and budgets. Transactions systems process the basic transactions of the firm; order entry, accounts receivable, and payables are all examples of this class of system. Weill was able to obtain figures for each firm's investment in these different categories of IT; six years of data for strategic, three years for informational, and one year for transactions. He also obtained data on six years of total IT investment.

Conversion effectiveness measures the ability of an organization to convert its IT investments into working applications. Not every development effort is successful, and management does not always take advantage of the opportunities that an IT initiative provides. Weill chose to measure conversion effectiveness in this study by ratings of top management commitment, experience with IT, user satisfaction, and the turbulence of the internal political environment.

Several performance measures are important in this study. Because a firm invests in strategic IT for competitive advantage, Weill collected data on the firm's sales growth rate and obtained market share data from the Valve Manufacturers Association. Informational investment is concerned with the goal of improving managerial decision making. An appropriate measure of performance here is return on assets, or ROA. Finally, companies invest in transactions processing systems to reduce costs. Weill calculated two performance measures: the number of employees who are classified as nonproduction (adjusted for sales) and the ratio of nonproduction labor to total employees.

The study tested a number of hypotheses about the relationship between IT investments and performance using different statistical techniques including correlation and regression analysis. The major highlights of the findings are as follows:

1. High investments in transactions processing applications are positively associated with high levels of ROA and labor productivity.

2. There were no positive relationships found between strategic IT investment and any measure of firm performance. In fact, high strategic investment was associated with lower labor productivity and growth.

3. Informational IT investment was not associated with any firm performance measures.

4. Firms with high conversion effectiveness showed a stronger, more positive relationship between strategic IT investment and firm performance.

These findings were among the first to relate investment in IT to firm performance measures. Although it would be nice to see evidence that all types of investment in IT correlated with performance, the reasoning in Chapter 1 suggests that such an outcome is unlikely. This study provides evidence to support the Investment Opportunities Matrix; some types of IT investment are more likely to result in a return than other types. The results on conversion effectiveness also support the IT value equation; a firm must be able to successfully implement technology if it is to obtain a return from its investment in IT.

As with all empirical research, questions of which variables are causal make interpreting the results a challenge. This research found that investment in transactional IT was associated with firm performance. Did the investment cause improvements in the return on assets, or did firms with higher returns decide to invest more in technology? A researcher can use various statistical techniques and logical arguments to argue for one particular view of causality, but the answer always remains tentative. Variables can be manipulated in a laboratory experiment to provide better evidence of causality, but then the setting is often artificial. In a company, investment and performance happen every year. Untangling the relationship among them, even with powerful statistical techniques, cannot prove the existence of a causal relationship. Research can, however, provide more and more evidence for you to take into account in deciding whether you believe IT contributes to improved performance.

Finding Value in Computerized Reservations Systems

The first airline computerized reservations system (CRS) solved operational problems; American Airlines was afraid its old, manual reservations system would break down with the advent of jet travel, because of the expected sudden increase in reservations. This concern led the airline to develop the famous SABRE on-line reservations system. The evidence for the contribution of this technology to the airlines is varied. Chapter 5 discusses some of the indirect returns from placing CRS terminals in travel agencies. This section presents historical evidence, based on the value and return to airline CRS subsidiaries, to support the argument that certain airlines have obtained a return on their investments in IT.

A computerized airline reservation system maintains a large database that contains the names of passengers associated with their flights. In the early days these systems were known as passenger name reservation (PNR) systems because the idea of keeping your name with your flight was so novel. These on-line systems removed the limitation of a manual, centralized reservations group. In terms of time and space, you can make a reservation anytime of the day or night from virtually anyplace in the world.

Airlines with reservation systems could also provide higher levels of service to their customers. They could better manage the airline because they had historical data on reservations and boardings. Using their reservation system as a base, airlines have added many functions ranging from listings of special dietary requests to balancing the loading of the aircraft.

Today one would have great difficulty starting up an airline without a reservation system. Donald Burr, chairman of Peoples Express, pointed out the lack of a decent reservation system as one of the factors that contributed to the demise of his airline. Peoples Express had too few reservation lines; it was not unusual for customers to be unable to reach them from early morning until late evening because of the number of callers. Southwest Airlines is the only major airline that has opted to stay out of airline CRS, or at least not to pay ticketing fees. The major CRS vendors, American and United, use this example when accused of antitrust violations. If the CRSs are an "essential facility," how can Southwest be successful without joining?

In recent years the airlines developed yield management systems; these programs look at future flights and dynamically adjust the number of special-fare seats depending on the number of reservations so far. American combines its yield management program with a discount-seat allocation program and an overbooking program. American estimates that during a three-year period, these systems generated quantifiable benefits including increased booking revenues of $1.4 billion. This number compares with American's profit of $892 million during the same period.

For several years the airline industry waited for an agreement on a common reservation system to be placed in travel agents' offices. Finally around 1976, United and American decided not to wait and began placing terminals connected to their systems in travel agencies. This move proved to be a tremendous benefit for both the agent and the airline.

The travel agent has become an extension of the airline's own reservations operation. Enhancements to the systems allowed agents to issue boarding passes with tickets. Thus, part of the boarding process has moved from the airport to the travel agency. Today some airlines are introducing electronic tickets; you do not receive a physical ticket and the airline does not have to process your ticket, saving considerable cost.

Each airline tried various approaches to using a CRS to increase its own bookings. First, the host carrier (the airline whose system is used by the agent) would list its flights first. That is, on American's SABRE system, American's flights between two cities always appeared first. Because over 90 percent of flights are booked from the first reservation screen, the host airline enjoyed a tremendous advantage.

Delta and other airlines complained about this inherent bias in computerized reservation systems. The U.S. Department of Transportation investigated and issued a series of rules requiring listings that did not unduly favor the host carrier. The carriers made the changes, grudgingly. By this time, American and United had spent well over $250 million each on their systems, and they felt they deserved the rewards from that investment.

Where does the return from these systems come from? When an agent using an American Airlines CRS books a ticket on Northwest, Northwest must pay American a booking fee of about $2.00 to $2.50 per leg. There is one story of a travel agent in Minneapolis who booked most flights on Northwest, but used the United Apollo system. In one year he generated $1 million in fees for United.

In some years, American's SABRE subsidiary has reported higher profits than the airline. At one congressional hearing, Robert Crandall, American's recently retired CEO, said that "if forced to break up American, I might just sell the airline and keep the reservations system." When TWA was last sold, one attractive feature was its reservation system. In 1996 American sold part of its SABRE subsidiary. The overall market value of American Airlines at the time was $6.2 billion; the initial public offering of SABRE valued the subsidiary at about $3 billion, nearly half the airline's market value.

There is a great deal of evidence that the major CRS vendors, particularly American and United (United is now a partner in Apollo, as it sold shares in its Covia CRS subsidiary to other airlines), have obtained a return from their investment in information technology. Unfortunately, the magnitude of their investment is not public information; industry estimates of investments over $1 billion or more for each system seem credible. Although we cannot calculate a rate of return, there is strong evidence that the CRS vendor airlines have obtained significant value from their investments in information technology.

Manufacturing Firms and IT

Productivity is most easily measured in the manufacturing as opposed to the service sector. A recent study looked at data for 60 manufacturing business units in the United States and western Europe for the period 1973-1984 (Loveman 1994). The researcher used different models of production functions to estimate the return on investments in IT capital. The study employed a variety of models all related to the contribution IT could make to productivity. According to Loveman (1994), "The data speak unequivocally: In this sample, there is no evidence of strong productivity gains from IT investments."

There are a number of possible explanations for this finding. First, the sample is from a time that preceded the rapid expansion of PCs. The author also suggests that the true returns may be very large, but that economists lack the tools to measure them. There may also be subtle organizational and strategic factors that reduce or hide the payoff from IT.

For this kind of study, when IT acts as a substitute for labor, a cost-benefit methodology is quite appropriate. However, when IT enhances the quality of a product by reducing cycle time or by adding value through service or information content, economic methods of analysis encounter problems. Similarly, it is very difficult to value enhanced information that IT might provide to decision makers. Information and technology also have to be integrated with the firm; management must figure out how to take advantage of new information or the features that IT has to offer. "The absence of a significant productivity effect from IT therefore must be seen... as a failure by managers to build organizations that effectively integrated IT with business strategy, human resource management, and efficient resource allocation" (Loveman 1994).

Would the results of this research be different with a more recent sample of firms? The results reported by Loveman are typical of most econometric studies of IT productivity across firms, with the exception of the research described in the next section.

An Optimistic Study Across Firms

Studies of the return on investing in information technology are relatively few, partially because it is so difficult to obtain data. Companies often do not track IT investments after they have implemented the technology. If they do, the firm often considers the data to be proprietary and will not release it.

Another way to study investment is to obtain aggregate data for firms from places like government studies, firms that collect and sell data, or from publicly available documents like annual reports. There are a large number of studies, often undertaken by economists, that deal with industrywide or economywide issues. One such study of IT investment produced results that led to stories in industry newspapers heralding the huge return firms get from investing in technology (Brynjolfsson and Hitt 1996), which we will discuss because it is so well known and often quoted. It is also important to discuss the credibility of the statistical findings, especially with reference to the discussion in Chapters 1 and 2.

The data in the study come from 367 large firms with almost $2 trillion of output during the period 1987-1991. Brynjolfsson and Hitt (1996) argue that economic theory holds that in equilibrium, companies that spend more on technology would not, on the average, have higher profitability or stock market returns than firms spending less. Managers would both overspend and underspend, so high spending would not necessarily be better. A high correlation between IT investment and stock price and profits would mean that IT was contributing an unexpectedly large amount to performance.

Instead of looking for simple correlations, Brynjolfsson and Hitt applied the economic theory of production functions to the search for IT value. A production function hypothesizes that the output of a firm is related to each of its inputs. The production function predicts that each input should make a positive contribution to output. The marginal cost of each input should just equal the marginal benefits it produces. Based on this theory, the researchers test two hypotheses: (1) Computer capital and staff make a positive contribution to firm output, and (2) this result holds even after accounting for depreciation and labor expense. The Cobb-Douglas production function comes from economics and is frequently used in this type of study. Brynjolfsson and Hitt constructed a system of equations for each of the five years in their study period.

The study employs data collected by the International Data Group (IDG) in its annual survey of IS managers in large firms. The researchers matched the firms in this study to financial information contained on the Standard and Poor's Computstat II files. The figure for capital was obtained by adding the IDG estimate for supercomputers, mainframes, and minicomputers and an estimate of the value of PCs and terminals. Appropriate price deflators were applied to the data The typical firm in the sample is large, with five-year average sales of over $7 billion.

The results of the study produce a gross marginal product for computer capital of 81 percent. The marginal productivity for computer capital is comparable to the marginal product of other types of capital. For each dollar spent on IS staff labor, the increase in output is estimated to be $2.62, a huge return from labor. An earlier version of this paper (Brynjolfsson and Hitt 1993) stated that the study found a return on computer investment of 54 percent in manufacturing firms and 68 percent in manufacturing and services combined. Looking at these results, a CEO would be advised to invest in nothing but technology! Brynjolfsson has written about the productivity paradox, and he now considers that, at least for these firms, it no longer exists.

It is possible to conduct empirical research with great care and rigor; in fact, researchers are obligated to do so to provide reliable and valid results. However, those who conduct studies also have to ask if their results "feel right." What do you think about the returns described earlier? How many individual investments in technology have you seen where the return is 50 percent? Is it likely that your firm could average a 50 percent return across all of its investment in IT?

What is going on here? First, the study is looking at capital invested in computers. In addition to this capital, one has to purchase software and communications equipment, two expenditures omitted from the study. The investments we have been discussing so far relate to actual applications of the technology; this study looks at computer capital and its contribution to output. Purchasing and installing a computer cannot really contribute to output; one has to develop and/or buy applications. It also requires labor to apply computer capital to developing a system. The study does find IS staff labor to be a very positive factor contributing to output. The authors try a number of sensitivity analyses to see if large errors in their data would make dramatic changes in the results. In general, the findings still indicate that computer capital and IS staff labor make a significant, positive contribution to output.

Why am I skeptical about these results? In Chapter 1 and with Weill's results in this chapter, we saw that returns are different based on the type of investment. In the Brynjolfsson and Hitt (1993) study, all types of investment are lumped together. Weill found a return from only one type, transactional. In Chapter 2 we studied examples of project failures and saw an estimate that more than 20 percent of IT projects may be canceled. These projects cannot possibly contribute to a positive output.

I have discussed the paper with economists and learned that typical returns to capital on real terms (adjusted for inflation) run 3 percent to 10 percent. Possibly the omission of software and communications costs are responsible for some of the high estimated returns from IT investment. The R^2 values in this kind of research measure the correlation between what the researchers' model predicts and the numbers in the actual sample; they range between 0 for no correlation to 1.0 for a perfect fit. Loveman has R^2 values ranging from 0.77 to 0.90, whereas Brynjolfsson and Hitt have values around 0.98. These latter numbers are extremely high; do they indicate a problem with the data or the model? How do we reconcile the failure to find strong returns in other research with a study that shows incredible returns from investing in IT, a study done with the best data yet available by two highly competent and respected researchers?

There are a number of possibilities. First, the Brynjolfsson and Hitt study is at a very macro level. It relates four independent variables, computer capital, noncomputer capital, IS labor, and other labor and expenses to sales. The model does not specify the mechanism by which these variables are related. Our approach to this point has been much more micro; we have looked at individual investments in technology and classified them by type. The examples in the book so far deal with specific applications like an airline CRS. In the production function study, there could be some other variable that is related to output, IS capital, and computer capital so that the relationship among them is less than what is suggested in the results. Another possibility is that highly successful companies spend a great deal on information technology; high sales generate the revenue needed to purchase computers and hire IS staff. In this case causality runs from output to investment in IT rather than vice versa. (Though Brynjolfsson and Hitt did some testing for causal direction and feel that the evidence is stronger for IT investment leading to firm performance rather than vice versa.)

Experience tells me that Chapters 1 and 2 and Weill's results are more credible than the results from this large-scale study. Although I would like to see a high return from IT investments, an average return (which must include failures and successes) of over 50 percent is more than most of us who have been working in this field for some time can imagine.

Risk Management in Commercial Banks

Banks face substantial risks in their trading operations. There have been a number of well-publicized examples where unauthorized trading has caused significant problems. In one case, the old-line firm of Barings lost so much from unauthorized trading in its Singapore office that the bank ended up being acquired by ING and disappeared as a separate entity.

NYU doctoral student Kathie Duliba (1997) recently finished a dissertation relating investment in risk management information technology to performance in bank trading. She collected data from the Federal Reserve on bank trading results for a six-quarter period. While the data cover only 19 banks, this group of banks is responsible for 93 percent of U.S. trading in the instruments she studied. Through in-person interviews she measured the functionality of bank risk-management systems, ranging from a possible score of 0 to 30 for a system with the highest degree of functionality.

One of the innovations in this research is to look at functionality rather than just the pure dollar amount invested in IT. Pat Harker at Wharton has conducted a large study of the productivity and efficiency of investments in information technology in retail banking. He reported finding no correlation between investment and the functionality of the systems in the study! This finding means that, for the same investment, two different banks obtained systems with widely differing functionality. It suggests that it is not how much you invest, but how well you invest that matters. This idea fits well with conversion effectiveness; you must succeed in turning an investment in IT into something useful if you are to obtain a return.

Duliba used a series of regression equations to look at the relationship between the functionality of risk management software and the banks' performance in trading during the six quarters for which data was available. Her results showed that functionality of the system was positively associated with revenues from trading interest-rate products, though it was slightly negatively associated with revenues from foreign exchange products.

The study design does not make it possible to determine the causal directions of the results. Do banks that are successful traders recognize the need for highly functional risk management software, or does the software enable them to conduct more trading and assume more risk? The answer is probably that both explanations are correct. The bank that wants to be successful in trading is motivated to develop risk management software; this software helps the bank to achieve higher performance from trading.

The first finding of an association between interest-rate product revenues and the functionality of the software is preliminary but important evidence. If other studies confirm the relationship between IT investment, returns, and the functionality of the IT application, then we have further evidence of why IT investment is not always associated with a return.

The results from Duliba and Harker say that IT investment provides a return that is contingent on the functionality of the IT application. How does one get functionality? Functionality comes from conversion effectiveness. It is not just spending money; the return from IT depends on how well the organization spends its money and how skillful it is in generating functionality from its investment.

A Two-Stage Approach

The banking risk-management study examined the trading process, arguing that the total economic performance of large banks consists of their performance in hundreds of aspects of banking. It measured the results from trading, not the performance of the entire bank. (Trading, however, is a major process with a number of steps.) A study of manufacturing and the impact of information technology during the 1978-1984 period also focused on process; this research is based on a model that relates investment in IT first to five intermediate processes, and then links these processes to overall performance (Barua, Kriebel, and Mukhopadhyay 1995).

The study used data from the Strategic Planning Institute in Cambridge, Massachusetts. For the 1978-1984 period, the Institute collected data on management productivity and IT. The researchers first examined the impact of information technology investment on five intermediate variables or processes:

1. Capacity utilization at the strategic business unit level

2. Inventory turnover

3. Relative quality

4. Relative price

5. Percentage of new products

The researchers tested their beliefs with regression models linking IT investment to these five intermediate variables above and with models assessing the impact of the five variables on market share and return on assets.

The first part of the analysis found a significant relationship between IT capital and capacity utilization, inventory turnover and quality, and a negative association with relative price, suggesting that IT investment helps reduce prices. IT capital was not significantly associated with percentage of sales represented by products introduced in the last three years. The second stage of the analysis found that all five intermediate variables had significant impacts on the economic output variables, market share, and return on assets.

The analysis provides evidence that IT investments have their primary impact at lower levels in the firm than the aggregate measures often used to evaluate firm performance. IT capital, particularly in manufacturing, is applied to business units and to processes in those units. If the results of this study are correct, we should find evidence of IT value at lower levels in the organization, particularly at the business process level.

Implications of the Studies

While we have by no means been exhaustive in reviewing every study of IT investment and return for multiple firms, it is safe to say that the results in this chapter are hardly overwhelming. These studies present the most favorable case. We have omitted some earlier econometric studies that showed no relationship between IT investment and performance. The results are summarized in Table 3-1.

Table 3-1

Summary of Industry Studies

Investment	Results	Observations
Valve industry study	Transactional IT associated with a positive return on investment	This study supports the contention that one cannot expect the same return from each type of IT investment
Airline computerized reservations systems research	For the CRS vendors, investing in this technology led to highly profitable subsidiaries	We do not know the level of investment to calculate a return; the extremely high market value of the subsidiaries suggests a positive ROI
Studies: 1. manufacturing firms 2. across 367 firms	1. No returns from IT 2. Very high rates of return from IT investment	Estimated return in second study seems too high based on experience
Risk management technology in banking	A positive relationship found between functionality of risk management system and revenue from trading	This study suggests that it is not just investment in IT, but how well the firm converts the investment into system functionality
Study of 88 manufacturing firms	IT capital is associated with intermediate business processes that, in turn, are associated with firm performance	The results support the argument that IT acts on firm-level performance through its impact on lower-level processes

The study of the valve manufacturing industry does support the argument that one cannot expect to find returns from all types of IT investment. Weill also contributes the notion of conversion effectiveness, which is important in the discussion in Chapter 2 about successful implementation of technology.

The study of risk management systems in banks offers some evidence for the importance of functionality; how you convert the investment in technology into an actual application is crucial. This study also provides evidence of an association between functionality and a measure of bank performance. The research focused on the business process, which is similar to the approach taken in the last study review of manufacturing firms.

Several studies in this chapter suggest that it will be difficult to associate the general level of IT investment with firmwide performance measures in many companies. Information technology frequently affects firm performance through a large number of individual applications, each of which may or may not show a return on investment.

The airline industry provides very broad data about the return from investing in reservations systems. However, the opportunities to make this kind of investment rarely occur. It is unlikely that anyone at American Airlines in the late 1950s understood how this investment would grow. In this instance, the rewards did accrue to the first movers; it would be difficult, if not impossible, to build a system like SABRE or Apollo from scratch today. However, these systems are threatened by the graphical interfaces and availability of the World Wide Web and by cheaper fares through auctions. American has responded by making EAASY SABRE available on the Net, and using SABRE as the underlying system for a travel-oriented Web site, Travelocity.

The large-scale econometric study presents a very optimistic picture of the return from investing in computer capital and the productivity of IS staff labor. These results are in the direction we would like to see, but possibly they are too far in that direction. The numbers are so large that I suspect most CEOs would discount them. Since the study is well done and follows accepted econometric techniques, it may quiet some critics who have complained that similar studies in the past have shown no relationship between IT investment and output.

It is surprising that we have found so few studies given the importance of the topic. With an estimated 50 percent of capital investment in information technology, why are there so few studies and such little evidence of measurable returns? Certainly one explanation is the quality of data available and the difficulty of collecting it. Researchers may also be discouraged by problems of demonstrating causal relationships given the dynamic business conditions that exist today. Whatever the reason, we shall rely more on the results of technology investment in individual companies rather than across firms in our search for IT value.

CHAPTER FOUR

IT Investments with Direct Returns

n the type of IT investment where a direct return is obvious, it should be relatively easy to compute a ROI. In this chapter, we describe one such application at Merrill Lynch in some detail. Most of the other examples demonstrate cost savings or revenue enhancement, but we do not know the level of investment required to generate these returns. This chapter demonstrates that it is possible to obtain a measurable return from IT, though for most examples in the book it is not possible to provide actual ROI figures.

A Securities Processing System

Merrill Lynch is the largest brokerage and financial services firm in the United States, with almost 50,000 employees and more than 500 branch offices. The objective of the securities processing operation is to receive certificates from customers, perform the proper processing of the certificates, and post data to customer accounts.

A very high-level process flow consists of the following steps:

1. The customer brings documents to a branch office

2. The branch does preliminary processing

3. Certificates are sent to a processing center

4. The center verifies and checks the certificates

5. The center processes certificates

6. The center posts data to the customer's account

On a typical day, Merrill Lynch offices around the United States receive some 3,500 securities that need processing of some kind. What are some of the reasons for customers bringing securities to a branch office?

1. The customer has sold the stock and must surrender it so that shares can be issued to the buyer.

2. A person has inherited stock and must have the shares registered in his or her name.

3. A company has reorganized and has called its old stock to issue new shares.

4. A bond has been called by the issuer.

5. A customer wants Merrill to hold his or her securities.

The customer brings the security plus other supporting documents to the branch office cashier. The cashier provides a receipt and batches all of the securities together to be sent for processing. Before the development of a new process, the branch sent these documents to one of two securities processing centers (SPC), either Philadelphia or Chicago.

The objective of securities processing at the centers was to credit the customer's account as soon as possible, certainly within the 24 hours suggested by the Securities and Exchange Commission. Because of exceptions and the possible need to contact the customer again, sometimes it was not possible to achieve this goal.

A good example of problems is in the area of legal transfers when someone inherits stock. There are requirements for supporting documents like a death certificate. If the customer does not bring the documents and the branch does not catch the fact that a necessary piece of paper is missing, the securities processing center must contact the branch and ask them to contact the customer.

Because many of the securities are negotiable, the SPCs must be extremely careful in processing. Merrill Lynch is required to keep an accurate audit trail whenever it moves a security. This requirement led to frequent, repeated microfilming of securities as they moved around a center.

To the Merrill Lynch financial consultant (FC) or broker, the securities processing task seemed to require an inordinate amount of time that led to numerous problems. (There are some 15,000 FCs at Merrill.) The branch operations staff had to monitor accounts continually to see if securities had been credited properly. FCs were forced to contact clients to obtain additional documents. There was a great deal of friction between the sales side of the business and the securities processing department.

All of these reasons plus the labor-intensive nature of processing led to a desire to improve securities processing. The most radical approach would be to "obliterate" the process entirely. Unfortunately, this option is out of the control of Merrill Lynch. Although there has been much publicity about "book entry" shares of stocks, a large number of physical shares of stocks and bonds are still in circulation. Obliterating the process would require industry and government cooperation to eliminate all physical certificates, replacing them with an electronic record. This solution would also require consumer acceptance and a massive effort to record electronically and eliminate all existing paper certificates.

After suggestions by the operations staff and extensive research, the systems group at Merrill proposed a new process using image technology to capture an image of the security certificate and related documents that accompany a transaction. The focus of the project was on work-flow redesign, not just the use of image processing. Work-flow redesign involved the closing of the two processing centers mentioned earlier and the development of a securities processing department at a single site.

In this old process, customers brought securities and supporting documents to a branch office or sent them to Merrill through the mail. This set of documents will be referred to as a "certificate." After receiving the certificates, the branch conducted a manual review for negotiability. If the certificates appeared not to be negotiable, the clerk told the customer what additional information was necessary to complete the transaction.

During the day, several branch clerks accepted certificates and accumulated them. At the end of the day a courier took all certificates to one of the SPCs. The clerks attached a manually prepared manifest to the package summarizing its contents.

Normally the package arrived at the SPC the next day. Upon arrival, an SPC clerk inspected the package and checked that its contents balanced to the manifest. The clerk contacted the branch office to resolve any discrepancies. All certificates that matched the manifest continued to the next stage in processing.

The first step after bursting packages was to microfilm all certificates. Next, clerks conducted a second negotiability review that is contingent on the type of transaction: legal or nonlegal. An example of a legal transaction is a stock transfer because the customer had inherited the security. Regulations require that certain documents accompany the security, for example, a death certificate for the person in whose name the security is currently registered.

If further review showed the certificate was not negotiable, it was segregated. A clerk logged this status into a Merrill Lynch securities control system. Once classified as negotiable, the certificate moved to a final holding area for distribution.

The SPCs sent 80 percent to 90 percent of the certificates directly to depositories. The remaining certificates were distributed to specialty departments in New York for further processing, for example, a department handles exchanges of stock necessitated by a stock split.

Why did this process entail frequent microfilming? Merrill must carefully control securities and credit them to a customer's account as soon as possible. Given the volumes of paper involved, microfilming became an integral part of the control process. Merrill must also pass audits by the SEC, which checks controls on securities processing.

Merrill completely redesigned the SPC process. As in the old process, customers bring securities to a branch office or mail them to Merrill. The branch cashier conducts a preliminary negotiability review supported by an expert system. This system helps the cashier determine negotiability status; it also prints a customer receipt and generates a document control ticket that travels with the certificates. The expert posts a record of the certificate to a computer file, including a unique identifier number for the transaction.

At the end of the day, clerks package all certificates to be taken by courier to the single securities processing center. The system generates a manifest sheet for the package and updates a manifest file so that it contains information on the shipment.

At the SPC, the staff first wands a bar code on the package to verify receipt. Clerks check the package against the manifest; if there is a discrepancy, they update computer files and the computer notifies the branch. Branch personnel have access to these files so they can check the status of processing of any security at any time.

Negotiability must be verified in the new process, both for legal and nonlegal documents. However, the presence of the expert system in the branches reduced the number of certificates arriving without the documents needed for negotiability by 50 percent for legals and 75 percent for nonlegals.

A major technological innovation in the process was the introduction of image scanning and character recognition for certain key fields on the stock certificate. The scanning system recognizes a reference number via the bar code on the control sheet accompanying the certificates. The system uses the reference number to access the computer record, which shows the scanner operator the certificates included in the transaction. The operator scans the certificates and any legal documents. At this point the images and physical certificates diverge.

The scanned certificate image undergoes a character recognition procedure to turn three areas of the image into characters that can be processed by a computer. This recognition process converts three important fields from image to character format: the CUSIP number (a unique number for each security assigned by the securities industry), denomination of the security, and security number. These three numbers are already recorded in the computer; recognition of the imaged fields is to establish rigorous control and provide assurance that the right documents have been scanned.

The recognition task is complicated by the fact that there are no standard formats for securities; the three fields may exist anyplace on the security. The recognition algorithm needs to know where to look for the fields it is trying to convert. This information comes from a template database that indicates where the three fields are located on the security. Merrill has developed a template for each CUSIP and date-of-issue combination.

The system performs the image-to-character conversion by referencing the image, overlaying the template, and executing the algorithm. If the converted character fields match the same fields from the computer, the system updates the computer files to show that scanning has been completed and stores the images for this transaction permanently to optical disk. If there is a mismatch between the converted characters and the computer record, or other nonrecognition, the system refers the transaction to key edit. There, operators examine the image and input data to unrecognized fields.

The staff takes the physical certificates for distribution to their final location. The system executes a procedure to provide routing orders for each certificate; it specifies a destination box for the certificate. When a user needs access to security information, he or she can retrieve the image of the security on a graphics workstation. There is no need to access the physical security, or to hunt through microfilm records, a process that could take as long as three days in the old process.

Table 4-1 lists the major changes from the Merrill Lynch SPC process.

Table 4-1
Evaluation of Certificate Processing

Changes in organization structure

The major organizational change was the elimination of two securities processing centers and the consolidation of all securities processing in a central site.

Changes in work flows and functions performed

There are many such changes:

Branch office input changes	Elimination of most microfilming
Branch office customer receipt	Legal negotiability work-flow changes
Anticipated receipt information	Imaging operation; scanning and key edit
Package receipt and bar coding	Retrieval of image rather than physical security

Interface changes

Branch office interface	Worker interface with scanning
Customer interface	equipment
	User interface retrieving images

Major changes in technology

Expert system to assist branch cashier receiving certificates

Incorporation of scanning to replace most microfilm and provide better control, including:

Scanners	Retrieval of scanned documents
Template definition	Modifications to existing control
Key edit	system
Computer facility with optical disk jukebox	

Impact

Improvements in customer service

Better customer receipt	High-quality images compared to spotty
More information captured at point of contact	microfilm
Broker can query system for status of processing	Reduction in up to three-day searches for microfilm to instantaneous retrieval
Better control	Significant cost reduction
Certificate level control	Reduction in research time

The reengineering effort resulted in the elimination of two processing centers and the creation of a securities processing department at a central site. The process supports major changes in tasks and work flow, beginning with the receipt of securities at a branch office. The interface to the process for all groups having contact with it has also been changed.

Technology changes include the expert system for the branch office input, scanners, a template library, character recognition from images, and optical disk storage. There have been significant increases in the level of customer service and the quality of support securities processing provides to the branches. There is much less handling of physical securities, and retrieval time for a certificate image is nearly instantaneous. The time to research a security has been dramatically reduced; from up to three days in the old process to virtually instantaneously in the new.

The new securities processing system has had a dramatic impact on resources:

Reduction of occupancy from two locations to one

Reduction in depository fees

Interest savings on receivables

Reduction of microfilm costs

Savings in security services

Reduction in staff of 168 positions, leaving a current total of 165 including temporary staff

The new process required an investment of approximately $3 million. The payback period for the investment was less than two years, which translates to a savings of around $1.5 million a year.

This example shows that it is possible to justify an investment in technology and obtain an actual payback from doing so. A payback period of two years for an investment represents a healthy ROI. The redesign was successful enough that Merrill was able to outsource the entire system and processing to a third party, something that it could not have done with its old system. Outsourcing should result in even greater savings.

EDI and JIT at Chrysler

A very careful study of electronic data interchange and just-in-time inventory at Chrysler provides one of the most compelling examples of direct benefits from investing in information technology (Mukhopadhyay, Kekre, and Kalathur 1995). EDI is a very important technology: It connects buyers and sellers, allowing them to process orders and payments electronically. Most EDI today is done in batch processing mode, that is, a customer sends an order to a supplier who batches it with other orders and processes them several times a day. EDI eliminates much paperwork that accompanies a traditional ordering system; someone keys information into a computer once, and the system transmits it so that rekeying by the recipient is not necessary. EDI also dramatically speeds the order process by moving information electronically rather than physically.

The study described here had access to a decade of data from Chrysler and its suppliers. Chrysler management wanted to reduce manufacturing and logistics costs and streamline operations to enable JIT to work. The researchers analyzed the impact of EDI on inventory, obsolescence, and transportation costs for the 1981-1990 period. They developed a model that controls for variations in the complexity of operations coming from volume, parts complexity, product mix, and model and engineering changes. The results of the study suggest that the savings from better information exchange are over $60 per vehicle at the average Chrysler assembly plant. Another $40 in savings comes from electronic document preparation and communications, providing a total benefit of EDI of over $100 per vehicle. For all of Chrysler's plants, extrapolating this figure means $220 million in savings at 1995 production levels.

Chrysler began its first EDI link with suppliers as early as 1969, but its first attempt had a number of manual steps. Its current systems began in 1984 with an application called the Supplier Delivery Schedule transaction sending shipping quantities to suppliers electronically. Chrysler management gave a directive to implement just-in-time manufacturing, and EDI was the information technology that would enable JIT. Chrysler's overall goal was to reduce the price of a vehicle by 30 percent.

Because suppliers and Chrysler were not well coordinated, the company had to keep large, expensive safety buffers at assembly centers. Shortages led to costly line stoppages. Chrysler has the largest percentage of its production outsourced, 70 percent, which is comparable to practices at Toyota. (GM at the time had only about 30 percent of its components outsourced.)

Chrysler allowed time for suppliers to develop their own EDI capabilities, but made it clear that future business depended on being able to communicate electronically with the company. Suppliers also benefited from the program as they received production information for a 10-day period, as well as long-term forecasts. Electronic communications was a necessity because for some suppliers, goods arrived at Chrysler's receiving area within 15 minutes of the order.

Better information allowed Chrysler to move from less-than-truckload shipments to a scheduled pickup route for suppliers, saving transportation costs. Reduced buffer inventory meant reduced labor, fewer "stock chasers," and less money tied up in work-in-process.

The researchers collected data from nine assembly facilities. Because the study encompassed 10 years, many changes occurred, complicating statistical analysis. The study looked at two parts of the investment; the first part of the project focused on benefits from electronic information exchanges between Chrysler and its suppliers, and the second focused on savings from using electronic documents over paper and manual document preparation and handling.

The first analysis focused on four cost categories in assembly centers:

1. Inventory holding costs

2. Obsolete inventory costs

3. Transportation costs

4. Premium freight

EDI should provide better inventory utilization and reduce obsolescence costs at the end of the year when new models enter production; there should be fewer write-offs at model change because the inventory ordered will better match production. Transportation costs were not maintained by plant, so they could not be considered in the first models. Chrysler incurs premium freight costs when there is a disruption in normal operations requiring the use of special deliveries to solve the problem.

Although there could be confounding factors during the time period, the study showed inventory turnover at the assembly plants increasing as Chrysler increased its volume of EDI transactions with suppliers. The analysis of the data indicate that EDI resulted in substantial savings in inventory costs from lower inventory balances and more turns per year. EDI also was associated with lower obsolescence costs and with lower charges for premium freight, as the researchers expected.

Using aggregate statistics and controlling for changes in transportation mix and prices, an analysis of overall transportation costs produced an estimate of a reduction of $7.19 per vehicle. Similarly, electronic document handling helps reduce paperwork costs. In 1988 Chrysler manufactured 2.2 million vehicles and exchanged nearly 7 million EDI transactions with its suppliers. Mukhopadhyay, Kekre, and Kalathur (1995) estimate that EDI saves over $38 per vehicle in document preparation and handling costs.

For a plant with a production volume of 200,000 vehicles a year, the results of the study produce an estimate of a little over $100 per vehicle savings from the investment in EDI. Extrapolating this figure companywide gives the $220 million in savings mentioned earlier. What is missing? We do not know what Chrysler had to invest to achieve these benefits. Since Chrysler has lately had the highest profits and best performance of the Big Three, it is unlikely that they overinvested in IT, but we have no proof. The savings are impressive, but our case would be stronger if Chrysler could provide investment data as well.

A Securities System

In 1988 Barclays de Zoete Wedd (BZW) introduced a system called TRADE for the automatic execution of small orders in U.K. equities (Clemons and Weber 1996). BZW provides terminal software and network connection to small brokerage houses and money managers throughout the U.K. These customers can access current market prices and execute trades at the best prices available for more than 1,400 stocks and 95 government bonds. In 1993 the system handled 3,400 transactions a day, which constituted half of the trades BZW executed.

The development of TRADE was made possible by the "Big Bang" on the London Stock Exchange, when the Exchange deregulated commissions in October 1986. As a result of this major change, trading has moved off the floor of the LSE to electronic, screen-based trading. The LSE runs SEAQ (Stock Exchange Automated Quotation system), which is based on the NASDAQ system in the United States. There are pages for each of the LSE's 3,000 listed securities that show the market makers and their bid and offer prices. The page also shows the number of shares the market maker is willing to buy or sell at these prices.

Brokers, however, conduct negotiations over the phone; SEAQ does not provide automated trading. Both the broker and the market maker must write a trading ticket to confirm the trade. These tickets then move to an archaic, paper-based settlement system. Processing small trades is very expensive for securities firms relative to the amount of commissions they generate. Clemons and Weber report that in 1988, 40 percent of the trades in U.K. equities market were for 1,000 shares or less, a size well-suited to automated trading.

BZW undertook an economic analysis before deciding to develop TRADE. The company had experience running a retail order room that handled trades for other, smaller brokerages throughout the U.K. A software developer estimated the costs of building the system, which would be created from off-the-shelf technology, leased lines, and a third-party network. The estimates were based on the following calculations:

Revenue:

0.25 × spread × average trade size × number of trades

Cost:

(£2 × number of trades) + Development and Installation amortization

The one-quarter of the spread as revenue was based on the firm's trading experience. The retail order room helped BZW estimate the number of trades; the firm forecast an increase in the small order market share as a result of the system. They also figured that 20 percent of U.K. brokerage firms would adopt the system. It was unlikely that BZW would capture 100 percent of the business from adopting firms; brokers like to have multiple sources and not depend on a single market-maker. BZW assumed it would double its share of business from installing firms.

The cost side was easy compared to revenues. The marginal cost of added trades of £2 was an ongoing operating expense. To this must be added system development costs and the costs of promoting and installing the system at customer brokerages. The initial investment was to be £600,000 (about $1 million).

A BZW manager constructed a spreadsheet with these estimates and performed sensitivity analyses to see how important the various assumptions were. The model did not include the anticipated response from the LSE itself and from other competitors. BZW did look at several risks including not finishing the system on time, which would raise costs and delay benefits. Another risk would be the London Stock Exchange itself, creating rules to restrict systems like TRADE.

Two unanticipated events happened after BZW made the decision to invest in TRADE. Volume in the market in 1988 dropped about 35 percent from its 1987 peak when BZW undertook its analysis. Second, bid-ask spreads in the most active 100 shares fell nearly 45 percent after deregulation. However, BZW felt that the sensitivity analysis would still have shown the investment to be worthwhile even if these events had been known.

The system captures order data, automates trade execution, and provides confirmation and routing for settlement. The broker requesting a quote for a security receives the best price in the market, which is good for 30 seconds. During this window, the broker can trade by entering a quantity of shares to buy or sell. After 30 seconds, the system accepts the trade if prices are the same. If the price has changed, the broker gets the new quotation and the 30-second clock starts again. The software runs on a PC in the client's office; in addition to the BZW connection, the PC can pass trade and settlement information to other customer computers. A typical brokerage firm would have to invest £3,000 to £4,000 pounds to install TRADE. BZW also provides its research on about 700 companies through the system.

There are two major competitors to TRADE. Another firm developed BEST ahead of BZW; this system processed almost 1,000 trades a day by the time BZW was ready to install its system. The London Stock Exchange began an automatic execution facility to allocate trades on a rotating basis among the market makers showing the most favorable prices. By 1995, however, TRADE was handling twice as many transactions as the two rival automated systems combined. By the end of 1996 TRADE handled 6,500 trades a day. There are 56 TRADE users out of a total of about 90 firms that are large enough to use the system, giving TRADE a market share of about 62 percent. BZW's share of the small trade business went from 11 percent to 20 percent between 1988 and 1991. One customer routes 85 percent of its trading volume to BZW. BZW has also seen an increase in the volume at its retail order room. TRADE orders cost about £2 compared to an average of £10-£15 for a telephone trade. The system improves the quality of service and reduces errors in processing a trade, especially mismatched orders.

By all indications, TRADE is a successful system. Did BZW obtain a return on its investment in this IT application? We do not have access to the investment model spreadsheet. However, BZW does claim that events described earlier reducing benefits would not have been enough to make the investment unattractive. The benefits appear to be at least what the company forecast, and there is no information about huge cost overruns. It seems safe to conclude that the direct returns from TRADE have exceeded its development and operating costs. However, we do not know by how much, nor can we say what the actual rate of return on the IT investment has been.

Pacific Pride

Pacific Pride, based in Salem, Oregon, operates a commercial vehicle fueling system. This system consists of a series of fuel stations across most of the U.S. West Coast, primarily in the Pacific Northwest. Pacific Pride's customers range from large trucking companies to small, local firms like the neighborhood florist. A typical fueling station has retail and commercial pumps on the same site (Nault and Dexter 1995).

The commercial part of the station has no attendant. A fleet driver inserts a plastic punched card into a card reader and keys in an identification number. He or she may also enter an odometer reading. The system collects data on the fuel purchase and the time and location of the transactions. Pacific Pride calls its system Cardlock. Each billing period, Pacific Pride sends customers an itemized statement including the card number, the driver ID, the fuel purchased, time, location, and the odometer reading, if entered.

The system appeals to customers because they are better able to control fuel costs and monitor refueling transactions. The driver does not have a choice of the serivce station; he or she must purchase from Pacific Pride. This level of control appeals to fleet operators, as they are reluctant to provide drivers with cash and an option of where to spend it on fuel (and possibly other items).

Pacific Pride bases its retail price on the price leader in the area, ARCO, and uses the retail price to set its commercial rates. As such, both retail and commercial prices respond quickly to competition. Pacific Pride provides service in addition to fuel; its networked service stations are available to fleet drivers 24 hours a day, seven days a week. The invoice provides the customer with information to monitor and control fuel purchases, reducing its transactions costs. Nault and Dexter (1995) estimate that Pacific Pride was able to charge an average price premium of $.0785 per gallon from January 1987 to June 1988. Commercial customers paid from 4.8 percent to 12.3 percent of their fuel costs for the added value of IT in the form of the Cardlock system.

In the case of Pacific Pride, IT increased the value of a commodity product to customers through convenience and control. These benefits let Pacific Pride charge a small premium for the combination of fuel plus service that it provided fleet owners. This premium represents a direct return to Pacific Pride from its investment in Cardlock, though we do not have information on the size of that investment.

When There Is No Other Way

The third category in the Investment Opportunities Matrix describes a type of IT investment for cases where there is no other way to accomplish some objective. What kind of system might fit into this category? American Airlines undertook the SABRE system in 1958 because it saw, with the advent of jet travel, that its manual procedures for making reservations would break down in the early 1960s. The company's conclusion: There is no other way to handle the volume of reservations we predict are likely unless we use a computer system.

The initial investment in a system to process reservations came to $40 million, the equivalent to the cost of four Boeing 707s. At a New York University seminar (November 3, 1992), Max Hopper, the recently retired vice president in charge of the SABRE system, said that purchasing the planes instead would have created a 20 percent increase in American's jet fleet. Today, SABRE has become a travel supermarket through considerable additional investment.

According to the SABRE Group Web site in May 1997, the system

handles 25 percent of the world's airline reservations, 20 percent of the world's hotel bookings, and 80 percent of U.S. car bookings;

provides travel agents with access to 50 million available airfares;

tracks 80 million passengers, 4,400 flights, and 200,000 meals every day;

inventories 28,000 parts on more than 600 aircraft around the world;

serves 28,000 travel agencies in over 70 countries;

operates from a $34 million underground secure computer center in Tulsa, Oklahoma.

SABRE's computer complex

handles as many as 4,600 messages per second;

handles as many as 65,000 data accesses per second;

has data storage capacity in excess of 10 trillion characters;

uses a data network in 71 countries with 22,400 ports.

It is hard to imagine any system that does not use technology providing this kind of service. Did American have to add all of these features? The "no other way" to make reservations part of this system justified the first investment. Once the airline had the basic SABRE system in place, American built on it to create applications that provide better service to travel agents and its customers and which generate revenue. The "no other way" system became a competitive application for American.

The Air Traffic Control system is another example of one in which there appears to be no other way to handle the volume of flights in the United States today except to use information technology. I hesitate to use this example because the ATC system has been severely criticized for mismanagement, poor investment, and obsolete technology. If one reads about the underlying equipment, it is a miracle that the system performs as well as it does today. The Clinton Administration stopped work on a modernization program, as mentioned earlier, because it was not proceeding according to plan, and in fact had been bypassed by newer technology.

Part of the problem with the ATC system is the need to operate in a highly political environment. There are strict rules on procuring computers and other equipment to assure fairness in bidding. While fairness is an admirable goal, for the FAA it has resulted in purchases taking so long that new equipment is obsolete the day it arrives! The problems with ATC can be viewed as an example of failures of conversion effectiveness. The General Accounting Office has sharply criticized the FAA for its lack of management oversight of the Air Traffic Control modernization program; for years the FAA has refused to hire and assign a high-level manager to devote full-time to this project. Given expenditures of multiple billions of dollars on technology, such a position seems justified.

What is the return on investment for ATC? It is possible to compute how much airlines spend because their aircraft are delayed on the ground and in the air, and because they must follow assigned routes rather than the shortest route to a destination. However, the government runs the ATC (though there have been proposals to privatize it), and there are many beneficiaries including the traveling public, airlines, air freight companies, package delivery firms, and others. I have never seen a reference to a cost/benefit study of investing in ATC technology: It appears to be the only way to provide a viable air transportation system in the United States.

We find another "no other way" system in the package express business. Suppose that you operated an overnight delivery service with a fleet of trucks and airplanes. You could, when the volume of deliveries was low, not track packages. Instead, like the U.S. Postal Service, you would rely on the address on the package to be sure it is delivered. However, unlike the Postal Service, all packages are to be delivered the day after pickup. Therefore, every day, the system fills up with packages, and by the next day the system should be empty until that day's pickups start to arrive.

Of course, things don't go perfectly, so every now and then there is a mistake; a package is lost, or it arrives late. Customers call to find out where an item is and when it can be expected. How would a manual system work? The person originating the shipment could complete a multipart form that is attached to the package or envelope being sent. The driver takes one copy and files it at the office where he or she drops the shipment, such as an airport. A worker pulls another copy at the arrival airport and files it. If a customer has a question, a customer services representative asks the to and from locations, and calls the airport offices to have someone check the files to see where the package might be. With this information, the agent can make a good guess about the package's location.

While requiring a lot of paper and filing, this manual system might work for a small service. However, if you are Federal Express and want to be the largest overnight and freight system in the world, such a manual system will break down under the high volumes you expect. The FedEx network ties together a claimed 99 percent of the global economy; its system links 211 countries and territories. FedEx provides next-day and two-day express distribution in countries that account for 90 percent of the world's GDP (FedEx 1996 Annual Report).

How could you track packages without information technology? Would you justify this investment on its return? A technology-based system provides few easily quantifiable returns. There will be better customer service, but hopefully only a minority of customers will have a problem and need to inquire about the location of their packages. You can advertise the system as a way to show that FedEx is technologically advanced, and you can use the system to monitor package delivery performance. My belief is that FedEx invested in this technology because it was the only way to provide the first-rate customer service that is expected of a company that aspires to be the leader in the express delivery business.

According to FedEx, it invests $1 billion annually in "customer-serving, productivity-enhancing technologies" (FedEx Web pages). It claims that this investment pays for itself in efficiencies. It would be interesting to see the analysis for both this ongoing investment and the original decision to deploy package tracking technology. Today's package control and tracking starts with the driver using a wand to read a bar code on the package label. From this point on, people handling the package "wand" the bar code, which records where the package is located. A customer can inquire about a package through a toll-free number or from the FedEx Web site on the Internet. FedEx also uses technology to exchange billing and payment information with its clients.

American and FedEx have built on systems that I believe were originally justified, not from an expected return on investment in IT, but by the fact that there was simply no other way to provide the service they deemed necessary. The Air Traffic Control system was mandated by Congress when it established the FAA and gave it the responsibility for controlling air travel in the United States. As the volume of traffic grew, the FAA also found that there was no way to provide adequate capacity in the control system for the demand from airlines, the military, and civilian aviation without investing in information technology.

These systems have or can be expanded to generate revenue and/or reduce costs. These extensions may very well show a positive return on the incremental investment required to achieve them. We shall talk more about the competitive aspects of systems like SABRE and the FedEx tracking application in Chapter 7. For "no other way" systems, I expect the initial justification is likely not to be based on ROI, though extensions may well be justified through an economic analysis.

IT That Fits Two Categories

The categories in the Investment Opportunities Matrix imply that a particular application of technology is of one type. Given the complexity and multiple purposes for which companies make IT investments, it is not surprising that some applications fit in more than one category. Indirect benefits often accrue from an investment in the direct return category. Similarly, there are instances of applications where IT is the only way to accomplish your objectives, and the required investment also shows a direct return.

The need to verify credit card transactions and approve them while the customer is waiting falls into this category. There is no other way to handle today's volume of purchases for merchants than to use automated verification devices; these devices also provide a return to the merchant on his or her investment.

VeriFone is a company that makes hardware and software for payment applications; it is the "transactions automation company." Originally when you made a credit card purchase, the store clerk looked up the number of your credit card in a printed booklet of cards that were over their limits or that had been reported stolen. Information was up-to-date as of the last printing of the book. The next step was to require the merchant to phone a remote processing center to get approval for a credit card charge, a process that could take 60 seconds or more.

VeriFone was successful selling a small device that reads credit card magnetic stripes and allows the merchant to key in the amount of the purchase. The device phones an authorization center, transmits information from the card, and then displays the authorization number from the remote processing site.

The elapsed time for this transaction verification is 5 to 15 seconds; it costs between $.05 and $.15 compared to $.60 using the telephone (Galal 1995). Fully electronic settlement follows the authorization and takes 24 hours compared to 7-10 days with a manual system. The merchant should experience direct savings from an investment in credit card verification devices.

For the credit card companies, there is no other feasible way to handle a large volume of transactions, verifications, and payments in a timely fashion. The capacity to process transactions is a constraint on the amount of credit card use. A manual system would be overloaded at today's volume of credit card purchases. The credit card associations like Visa and Mastercard would have to raise the stores' limits (the threshold price at which authorization is required) and risk more bad debts because merchants and customers would not accept the waiting times for verification. Merchants would have lengthy waits for reimbursement. There is no other way but through the credit card association's investment in IT to create a smoothly operating payments system relying on credit cards. This same argument applies to debit cards, where the transactions involve transfering funds from the customer's account to the merchant's. Each account is likely to be in a different bank, and it is the credit card association system that must connect both parties to complete the transaction. Whether or not the credit card and debit card systems showed a direct return, the associations had no choice but to develop them.

Summary

This chapter has dealt with the easiest type of IT investment for finding value: One that is motivated by an expected direct return from the technology initiative. We have also discussed systems where technology is likely to be justified because there is "no other way" to solve a problem or provide a service. Direct systems are the ones that most people have in mind when looking at a traditional return on investment calculation for justifying an IT investment. See Table 4-2 for a summary of the investments discussed in this chapter.

Merrill Lynch justified its SPC system on an economic return; they achieved a payback period of less than two years. Chrysler made its investment in technology for EDI and JIT production as a way to achieve a 30 percent reduction per vehicle in the cost of manufacturing. Backing into a return calculation, a number like 30 percent should justify a fairly large investment in technology! The results from this investment are very impressive. Similarly, BZW undertook a rigorous analysis of the TRADE system before committing

Table 4-2

Summary of Investments with Direct Returns

Investment	Results	Observations
Merrill Lynch SPC system	Invest $3 million for less than two-year payback	Good example where we know investment and payback
Chrysler EDI	Save $100 per car for systemwide savings of $220 million	We do not know investment, but suspect it was less than benefits
BZW trade system	Electronic trading system for correspondent brokerage firms	Led to increase in business of small trades for BZW; $1 million investment appears to have a positive return
Pacific Pride	Automated refueling depots provided customers with convenience and control	Allowed company to charge higher prices for fuel plus service
SABRE	No other way to handle reservations when jet travel began	System that American had to develop became a competitive advantage for the airline
Air Traffic Control system	No way to handle today's volume of flights manually	The federal government made the investment for the system; the benefits accrue to flying public, airlines, private aviation (the total value has not been estimated)
Federal Express	Investment in IT the only reasonable way to track packages; today FedEx claims to invest $1 billion a year in technology to improve service and productivity	Some savings are likely for customer service; new investment for productivity enhancement should be able to show direct return; customer service investments more difficult to evaluate
VeriFone and credit card companies	Systems to improve verification; IT the only way to handle today's volume of business	Easy to calculate benefits to merchant from VeriFone products; for Visa, MasterCard, Amex, Discover, etc., technology allows increasing volume of transactions; the return is removing constraints on growth

to its development. While the exact numbers are unavailable, it appears that there has been a return from this investment.

Systems with a direct return are closely related to applications like credit card processing and air traffic control, where there appears to be no other way to solve a problem than investing in information technology. As the technology becomes more and more pervasive, systems that fall into the "no other way" category will be found often. If the organizations with whom one does business employs technology heavily, you will be forced to invest in technology to connect with them. In many instances, you will have little choice. If a major customer says that you must be able to accept electronic orders to keep its business, you invest in the technology or you lose a customer!

The examples in this chapter are an important part of our claim that one can find measurable value from investments in information technology. It would be nice to have more concrete numbers, but the results look positive even without a complete accounting. At the micro level of individual firms and applications, the examples in this chapter present clear evidence that there is value from investing in information technology.

PART III

Indirect and Less Obvious Returns from IT Investment

ndirect returns are largely unanticipated. A firm may invest in technology to automate its order entry to save money by having customers enter their own orders. This application has the indirect benefit of reducing the order cycle time because customers do not have to wait for the mail to transmit an order. If customers like the convenience provided by the order system, they may become more loyal to its developer and give the firm more business. Such a reaction by the customer is an example of an indirect benefit. These benefits are difficult to envision and evaluate when an IT investment is first suggested, but they can provide significant value for the firm.

This section includes consideration of infrastructure, the information technology platform that enables a variety of IT applications. A network is an example of infrastructure; it is available for a variety of uses. We present examples of infrastructure that have enabled organizations to undertake new initiatives. Since you do not always know the use for infrastructure in advance, justifying investment in it is challenging.

What is the value of an IT investment that becomes part of the firm's strategy? How is the contribution of this investment evaluated when the firm itself changes its strategy to build on the value provided by the technology? Chapter 7 contains examples of firms that have recognized the value of their IT investments and changed their strategies to take advantage of new opportunities it provides.

Another reason to invest in IT is to enable change, to transform the organization. Most of the time, these investments will be part of a general change program. Chapter 8 provides examples of five companies where information technology has had an impact on organizational structure. Two companies used IT to help design themselves, and another used technology to help it become a global, virtual firm. In a final example, a Danish firm invested in technology to help realize the chairman's vision of a team-based organization. In each of these firms IT delivered value, but the companies would have a difficult time calculating a return on investment figure.

CHAPTER FIVE

The Indirect Benefits from IT Investments

What are indirect benefits from an investment in IT? Indirect benefits occur from a second-order effect of the technology, and often these benefits are unanticipated when the original technology investment is made. Table 5-1 describes some ways in which indirect benefits accrue to the firm that innovates with IT.

Table 5-1
Indirect Benefits of IT Investment

Source of Possible Indirect Benefits	Examples
Making it easier to do business with the innovator	Developing an EDI capability to encourage customers to select the innovator as a supplier
Encouraging business by using technology to create a positive impression of the firm	FedEx Web site for tracking packages may encourage customers to use FedEx for more shipments because of its convenience
Using IT to provide outstanding customer service	McKesson helped its independent drug-store customers withstand the threat of drug chains through a variety of initiatives
Using IT to create biased markets	Baxter's order entry system in hospitals

In each of the examples in Table 5-1 a system has had a second-order impact for its developer. An EDI capability saves ordering and order fulfillment costs; it also makes a firm with EDI capability easier for a customer to use. The FedEx Web site is very impressive. The company will reduce costs through less use of its 800 customer service number and the need for fewer service agents. FedEx should obtain indirect benefits as the site encourages customers to place more business with the carrier. McKesson developed its Economost system to reduce its costs and increase volume; by providing superb customer service and innovative programs for its pharmacy customers, it helped keep these independent stores in business. Finally, indirect benefits accrue from *biased markets,* a result of many proprietary order entry systems. Customers find these systems easy and attractive to use; the innovator biases the market by featuring its own products only or by giving them preference. The early airline CRSs were accused of being biased when the CRS vendors listed their own flights first.

It is not easy to classify IT investment as direct or indirect without knowing the original justification for the IT initiative. The indirect benefits in Table 5-1 were probably not anticipated when the companies made their original investments; these benefits would certainly have been difficult to forecast *a priori. In general, the greater the distance in business process terms between where the investment occurs and where benefits appear, the more likely that the benefits are "indirect."*

The Case of Airline CRSs in Travel Agencies

The airline industry provides an opportunity to assess the indirect benefits of investing in IT. One of the major milestones in the history of CRS investments came when American and United began to deploy terminals to travel agencies. The CRS vendor would gain by creating a biased market favoring its flights. Expanding the system to travel agents also required including more capabilities in the system like the ability to reserve rental cars and hotel rooms. The CRS system itself became such a highly specialized asset for its vendors that airlines needed to offer further innovative travel services.

In 1976 United and American began installing terminals, connected to the airlines' computerized reservations systems, in travel agents' offices (Copeland and McKenney 1988). Several other airlines quickly imitated their behavior. Airlines already received direct benefits from booking fees and charges to travel agents and obtained indirect benefits through biased markets and outstanding customer service.

Many of the indirect benefits described earlier are enjoyed by all airlines whose flights are listed in a CRS. What are the indirect benefits that accrue to the *owner* of a system? One example is extra bookings due to screen bias, as mentioned earlier. Until it was eliminated by government regulation in 1984, CRS vendors routinely listed their own flights first on the reservations display. Since it has been estimated that over 90 percent of flights are booked from the first screen, this bias favored the airline. Even though rules by the Civil Aeronautics Board (CAB) at first, and later by the Department of Transportation, attempted to eliminate screen bias, non-CRS vendors have continued to assert that subtle biases in systems favor CRS vendors

Another indirect benefit for the CRS vendor is the "halo," which is a tendency to book more passengers on the flights of the airline that supplies a travel agency's reservations than would otherwise be the case. This favoritism might come about because of more familiarity with the airline and contact with its personnel, a favorable impression of the airline created by its technological capabilities, or the overall benefits of the CRS for the agent. As deployment of the technology reaches a critical mass, these benefits become more likely to occur.

We have conducted an in-depth study of the deployment of airline CRS in travel agencies focusing on the indirect benefits received by the CRS vendors (Duliba, Kauffman, and Lucas 1997). Extensive access to data was required to perform this research. Estimates of the number of travel agencies using each vendor's CRS were made available by Copeland (Copeland and McKenney 1988). A. E. Sharpe, a provider of airline statistics furnished data on a variety of airline performance indicators, and BAR and LNA (providers of data on advertising) let us access their records of airline advertisements. A California market research firm provided information for a five-year period on CRS locations in travel agencies in various cities.

The project tested two models, a market share model and a national model of airline performance. Our reasoning was that having one's CRS in a large number of travel agencies would lead to an increase in air traffic market share between that city and others; this increased market share would then be evident in overall airline performance. Our test is of *indirect* benefits, as we removed from the data the ticketing fees that airlines pay to the CRS vendor for making a reservation.

We used a market share model (technically, a multinomial logit market share model) and tested it with data from a five-year period for 72 city-pair routes. In this regression analysis, the coefficient for the number of travel agencies where a CRS vendor's equipment was in use was highly significant. The model itself predicted market share as a function of advertising, number of departures, the average fare, whether or not there was a strike, and the previous year's total of CRS locations in travel agencies. (We chose the previous year because it takes time for the agent to learn to use the system and because we could not tell from the data exactly when in the year the agency installed CRS terminals.) These results indicate that for the city-pairs in our sample, having more travel agencies using a vendor's CRS was associated with an above-average market share for flights originating in that city.

At the national level, we also used regression models to look at the relationship over 12 years between CRS locations (also lagged one year), number of departures, average stage length (length of the average flight), and advertising expenditures with three dependent variables: airline load factor, revenue passenger miles, and operating profits. In the equations predicting each of these three dependent variables, the CRS location variable was positive and significant. Our conclusion is that having more travel agencies using a vendor airline's CRS is associated with better performance measures at a national level.

There is always the possibility that airlines which perform well chose to invest in CRS and to deploy their systems to travel agencies. We tried various statistical techniques to see if this explanation is better than one suggesting that indirect benefits arise from investing in IT. We cannot prove that IT investment causes better outcomes rather than vice versa, but the evidence is in favor of our explanation. Larger airlines such as United and American have the dominant market share in terminals deployed to travel agencies. They also have been the largest and most financially successful airlines. We believe, based on this study, that American and United had the resources to invest in IT, and that they obtained significant indirect benefits from their investment in travel agency automation.

Thirty Years of IT Leading to Allegiance

Allegiance is a new company that was formed in 1996. In many respects, however, it is an old company that has gone through a number of major changes. Allegiance began as American Hospital Supply (AHS), the largest hospital supply company in the United States and one of the few distributors with a nationwide presence. American Hospital Supply was the company first credited with extending its order entry system to customer locations; they began a trend that changed order entry and their industry.

AHS is an old story; however, the indirect benefits of this company's long-term investment in IT has not been stressed enough. Very few question the direct benefits that AHS attained with its order entry systems; the firm made it easier for customers to order from it and reduced its own order processing expenses.

The history of technology investments at AHS and its successor firms demonstrate that there are significant indirect benefits from IT. Because this company has such a rich history of IT investment, it shows how indirect benefits have grown over time. We will begin our review of AHS in 1963 (Short and Venkatraman 1992). Stanford University Hospital was a major AHS customer; the supply company was having trouble processing orders fast enough to avoid stockouts at the hospital. The sales staff came up with the idea of giving prepunched cards to the hospital to use in reordering; the hospital transferred the cards using a reader and phone lines to AHS. AHS punched duplicate cards, which it entered into its order processing system. This early generation system reduced order cycle times.

Soon, other customers heard about the system and requested it. By 1967 AHS offered its ASAP 1 system, which used a touch-tone telephone along with bar-code readers and prepunched cards. By 1973 ASAP 2 featured a teletype terminal at the hospital so that it could obtain a printed verification of its orders. ASAP 3 in 1981 provided customized services for the hospital; the hospital could create standing orders and use its own stock numbers, which the system translated into AHS's product numbers. In 1983 customers could connect their computers to the AHS order processing computer directly to accelerate purchasing. A PC that could be used off-line to enter orders was introduced in 1985; this technique reduced line charges.

Another major event occurred in 1985. AHS, deciding that its basic business was characterized by slow growth, proposed a merger with Hospital Corporation of America. This merger created a storm of protest from AHS customers. HCA was a for-profit chain of hospitals; AHS customers at nonprofit hospitals saw their purchases subsidizing HCA's hospitals, possibly even contributing to the construction of a new for-profit hospital in their service area. Some customers contacted the chairman of AHS and threatened to stop purchasing from the company. At this point, with things not going well, Baxter International purchased AHS to save it from an unfriendly takeover. One of the major attractions for Baxter was ASAP; the company suspended its own effort to develop a comparable system and put all of Baxter's products onto the AHS system.

In 1986 Baxter's ASAP 8 introduced electronic invoicing and funds transfer. By this time, however, customers were complaining about biased markets and the proliferation of order entry systems. Other suppliers also wanted to have the hospitals enter orders on-line. The hospital could have multiple terminals or, at a minimum, the need to learn and use several different order entry interfaces. A biased market exists when the technology encourages the customer to purchase one vendor's products over another's. Clearly ASAP fit these conditions; one of its major goals was to encourage customers to purchase from Baxter.

It was clear that the trend was to move away from biased markets. ASAP Express was Baxter's answer in 1988. Now Baxter, using a PC EDI package, would accept orders for many different vendors. Orders for Baxter products would be processed as before by Baxter. ASAP Express would pass orders for other vendors to a value-added EDI services firm, where they would be placed in the foreign vendor's EDI mailbox for processing. Baxter maintained that it would not take sales or marketing data from these orders that it passed through to other vendors. ASAP Express was a great success, with some 2,300 hospitals using it to reach 1,500 vendors by 1994 (Marshall 1995).

One major problem with ASAP Express was its proprietary nature; the system was closed in a time of open architecture. ASAP was also rapidly aging and becoming a legacy system, one that was hard to maintain and expand. To move to the next generation, Baxter developed the OnCall system with Bergen Brusweig, Eastman Kodak, Boise Cascade, and TSI International Software. This system had as a major objective replacing the paper trail accompanying the interaction between hospitals and suppliers. For the first time, Baxter would use the ANSI X.12 standard for EDI. (Part of the motivation was a federal mandate that hospitals had to switch to X.12 [Marshall 1995].)

In 1996, Baxter spun off its hospital and cost management services company to its stockholders. The new company, named Allegiance, contains much of the original AHS. This new structure is designed to let Baxter grow more quickly, and to focus Allegiance on the changes that are moving the U.S. health system to managed care. Is there a hint of technology in Allegiance's new business venture?

Before answering this question, we need to discuss the interplay of technology and business through AHS, Baxter, and finally Allegiance. The direct benefits of IT are fairly clear. What are the indirect benefits from over 30 years of IT investment? First, it is difficult to assign all of the events we are about to describe to technology alone. AHS has always had a superb logistics system. The various versions of ASAP were successful because AHS was able to deliver what the customer ordered. Without this capability, users would soon lose faith in ASAP and stop using it. ASAP fit within the existing capabilities of AHS and was successful because of them.

Early in the history of the system, it became clear to marketing and other managers at AHS that they had a resource that went beyond taking orders. With an electronic connection to the hospital, they were in a position to sell services as well as supplies. Hospitals have always been under cost pressures, though they have gotten more severe in the 1990s. Instead of just selling supplies, AHS saw itself as selling supplies and services to its customers. This strategy led to the development of new services that became products for hospitals. A preferred-vendor program encouraged hospitals to select AHS as the prime supplier in return for discounts, software, and consulting. AHS developed software to help a hospital manage its own inventories and, of course, to reorder from AHS.

In 1990 Baxter introduced its ValueLink program, an integrated logistics management system for hospitals tied to Baxter. The system features Baxter as the prime vendor; the hospital makes consolidated purchases electronically. Baxter delivers to multiple locations in the hospital several times a day, if necessary. In essence, Baxter has created Chrysler's just-in-time inventory system for its customers.

This new conceptualization, partially from the company's long history of IT investment, can be seen on Allegiance's Web page:

> More than any other company in health care, Allegiance Corporation can help hospitals and other providers manage their costs and resources. We can address the 20-plus percent of a hospital budget that goes for supplies, and the additional 20 percent or more that very often is devoted to managing those supplies.

IT investment, in combination with a logistics system and alert management, has changed a provider of hospital supplies to a company that manages costs accounting for a significant percentage of its customers' overall budgets.

Changes Through Groupware

Our next example is from a company that obtained indirect benefits from an investment in groupware, software designed to facilitate the work of individuals with a shared task. The company in this example is a software vendor itself and has a pseudonym of "Zeta Corporation." It has about 1,000 employees and revenues of $100 million. Zeta is located in the Midwest and has field offices throughout the world. It is one of the top 50 software companies in the United States. The company sells a variety of software products that run on different computing platforms. Zeta has a 53-person department of customer support to provide technical support for customers using the telephone (Orlikowski 1996).

Telephone support requests are often complex; the person taking the call may have to consult reference material and other support staff members. When a consultant identifies a bug, he or she sends it to the responsible product department. Because Zeta has introduced a number of new products, the demands on customer support are increasing; the group receives 100 phone calls on an average day. The consultants work four-hour shifts, so that about 20 are on the phone in any given day.

In 1992 Zeta installed Lotus Notes for the purpose of tracking customer calls. Orlikowski studied the changes employees made in response to Notes; she argues that the technology enabled but did not cause the changes she observed. Rather, the customer service department staff members improvised and adjusted to Notes, learning how to take advantage of its capabilities to improve the quality of their work. The researcher analyzed, in five phases, the changes in work that took place:

Phase 1:

Consultants enter calls into the Notes database while on the phone with customers, though in practice most recorded the calls on paper for later entry.

Electronic documentation of problems and progress. Consultants update the electronic record of a problem as they conduct research and resolve it. This feature allowed consultants to report accurately to customers what was being done about their problem, sheltering them from angry customers.

Managers began to use the database to monitor consultant performance; criteria for evaluation changed to include the quality of documentation of customer problems.

Norms emerged as to what should be included in documentation to make it useful for later reference.

The consultant's work became more public because it was available to everyone who accessed the database.

Consultants began to use the database to search for a prior resolution of the problem they were currently dealing with as soon as enough cases existed in the database. They reported resolving 50% of their problems through electronic searching as the database became "increasingly valuable over time." By 1994 the database contained 35,000 incident records.

Phase 2:

The workforce split formally into "front line" and "back line" consultants; junior consultants took calls first and resolved as many as possible by searching the database. Incidents they could not resolve they sent electronically to a more senior consultant for research. Work now became a shared responsibility.

The junior consultants were uncomfortable assigning work to senior colleagues, so management created intermediary positions for two senior consultants who reviewed calls and made the assignment to senior consultants when appropriate.

Phase 3:

Consultants began to interact more with each other electronically using Notes' email capability.

Consultants began to review the database and offer assistance on incidents they saw were still open; the specialists engaged in electronic help giving whether or not it was requested. Fortunately, the strong norm of customer service made proactive collaboration acceptable in the department.

Phase 4:

The firm extended the system to overseas offices, replicating the databases every two or three hours among the offices so that each had access to the other's incident database. There were some problems integrating the overseas offices since the consultants there had not been involved in building the original database.

The company developed similar systems based on Notes for tracking bugs in the product development departments.

Phase 5:

A number of people at Zeta wanted access to the database, and management had to institute access controls to respond to fears of the consultants that the information in the system could be abused.

Partially as a response to the requests above, consultants began to disseminate information from the database electronically in order to share the knowledge contained in the system. They generated sanitized summaries of information about common or difficult problems and their solutions, and shared them widely within the firm. (Orlikowski 1996)

This description of the introduction of new technology at Zeta demonstrates how the indirect benefits from investments in IT accrue over time. Notes enabled the customer service department to provide better support for customers, become more efficient through the ability to search for similar past problems and their solution electronically, and share knowledge throughout the firm. Orlikowski does not attempt (nor in all liklihood did Zeta) to assign a monetary value to these benefits nor to look for an ROI on the firm's investment in Notes. It is clear that the firm enjoyed substantial indirect benefits from its investment; the call-tracking application changed the nature of customer support. Did Zeta receive value from its investment and does that value exceed its cost?

The World Wide Web

A skeptic might argue that the only possible benefit from a Web site is indirect, since no one has figured out how to make money from this technology yet! While such a statement is not completely justified, there is some truth to it. Some companies offering services on the Web claim to be making money. Others selling products are generating revenue, but are not profitable yet. One of the most successful examples of this stage of development is the bookseller Amazon Books. The company has substantial sales, but by 1998 has yet to show a profit.

For a retailer like Amazon, a payments firm like First Virtual, or an Internet commerce company like OpenMarkets, the Internet is a part of their business. One would expect eventually these firms would obtain direct returns from their IT investments. What about companies for whom the Internet is an additional channel for providing information? Do these companies obtain any benefits from their investment? If so, are the benefits direct or indirect?

Otis Elevator, a subsidiary of United Technologies, is an excellent example of a firm that has obtained direct and possibly indirect benefits from its investments in technology. Otis is the world's largest elevator company, with over 68,000 employees in more than 1,700 worldwide locations. A U.S. $5.3 billion organization, Otis sells, manufactures, and installs over 41,000 elevators and escalators annually, and its mechanics and agent representatives maintain nearly 1 million elevators and escalators in almost every country of the world. It has more than 1.2 million elevators in operation, for some 370,000 new-equipment and service customers.

Although Otis is headquartered in the United States, over 80 percent of its employees are of nationalities other than American, and 85 percent of revenues are generated outside the United States. Its European and transcontinental operations contribute more than 50 percent of total sales volume, with North American operations responsible for about 25 percent. Pacific-Asian operations represent 19 percent, and the balance is derived from Latin American operations. One out of every four elevators sold in the world annually bears the Otis name.

Otis gearless elevators service the high-rise market, and more than 60 of the world's 100 tallest buildings have Otis high-rise equipment. For the midrise market of about 5- to 20-story buildings, Otis's geared products offer the same modular control structure and dispatching capabilities as its gearless counterparts. Otis elevators for low-rise buildings are low-cost hydraulic models. Otis also markets escalators, Trav-O-Lator moving walks, and the Otis Shuttle horizontal transportation systems.

Elevator modernization is a $3 billion worldwide market in which Otis is a player; Otis modernization sales have grown at a compound annual rate of more than 20 percent over the past five years. In addition, over 22,000 Otis mechanics maintain nearly one million elevators, escalators, and moving walks worldwide.

Otis is famous in IT circles for its OTISLINE system, which was installed in the 1980s. This system keeps a record of all service calls on the elevators Otis services. A customer calls the OTISLINE support center to request a service call; dispatchers there use the system to send a repair person.

At the completion of the service call, an operator enters the nature of the problem and the solution into the database. As a result, Otis has a complete history of the servicing of its elevators. Management can use the system to locate elevators that are having a particular problem and to look for signs of design or quality problems.

Otis also offers a remote elevator monitoring product, or REM. A chip built into the elevator diagnoses its performance. If it senses any problems, the chip uses a dedicated phone line to notify an Otis computer that it needs service. The former president of Otis, who is now chairman of United Technologies, indicated in an interview that his objective was that someday a customer would never have to be concerned about elevator service. The elevators would never break down because they would be smart enough to know when they needed service, and would summon a service technician.

Otis has a well-designed Web site at www.otis.com. Unlike some sites, Otis does not take orders through the Web. Why? Elevators are relatively expensive and tend to be custom-built for a building. There is a huge difference between selling books and elevators! Why, then, does Otis bother maintaining a Web site? What is the direct value from this investment? The Web site features a great deal of information about Otis. There is a history of elevators with illustrations. You can find information about each of Otis's products. A contractor can see schematics of how to prepare a building for the installation of an elevator.

There is very little possibility of Otis obtaining a direct benefit from this site either in terms of cost reduction or revenue generation. However, the firm may obtain indirect benefits through the information it provides to the public and to potential customers. It is possible for the architect or designer to download CAD (computer-aided design) files of the elevators. This Web site may make it easier to do business with Otis, and it certainly does a good job of communicating a picture of the company to the public and United Technology shareholders. Try browsing this Web site (www.otis.com) and see if you agree that any benefits for Otis from this investment in IT must be indirect.

Summary

The category of indirect benefits from investments in IT can be difficult to identify. We suggest that the further the benefits are from the original justification for the system, the more likely they are to be indirect. Because it is difficult to anticipate these indirect benefits, they are very hard to include in the jus-

Table 5-2

Summary of Investments with Indirect Benefits

Investment	Results	Observations
CRS in travel agencies	Study found substantial, indirect, nonfee performance associated with having a vendor airline's CRS in a travel agency	Do not know how much the airlines invested in this technology and cannot calculate a return
AHS-Baxter-Allegiance	Thirty years of IT investment changing the nature of firm's strategy and products	Do not know total investment; extensive use of IT suggests considerable indirect benefits from this investment
Zeta Corporation	Implementation of Lotus Notes for call tracking resulted in substantial changes in the nature of customer service	There was no attempt to value the indirect benefits from the application, nor do we know the initial investment
Otis	Presence on the Web does not appear to generate revenues	Provides substantial information to public, shareholders, contractors; benefits appear to be indirect

tification for an IT investment. For the airlines it is clear that the indirect benefits of travel agency automation were not foreseen (nor were they probably foreseeable) when the companies performed their initial justifications for the CRS application. At Baxter, the indirect benefits of its order entry system became evident, and the company built on them. Over time, the technology helped alter Baxter's strategy and led to the creation of Allegiance as a cost management firm. See Table 5-2 for a summary.

Indirect returns are hard to identify when planning an IT investment. As the airline example shows, they have a tremendous upside and can lead to substantial gains from an investment in IT. The airline CRS and Baxter add to the building evidence that there is value from investing in technology. While we cannot prove that the technology caused the results that we found in our study of travel agency automation, the data are encouraging.

Examples from Otis and many others suggest that companies believe there is some value from having a presence on the Web. For many firms, this value can only be indirect. While the benefits are unlikely to be obvious when justifying an initiative, the category of indirect benefits has the potential to produce substantial value from investing in IT.

CHAPTER SIX

Investing in the Infrastructure

Most people would agree that interstate highways and railroads are a part of the country's transportation infrastructure. Transportation is vital to the economy; it makes the movement of goods and people possible. Economic infrastructure provides a foundation on which to build commerce. Is there a technology infrastructure? At the national level, there is a communications infrastructure in the form of networks that carry voice and data traffic. In recent years, the Internet has become an infrastructure that ties a wide variety of computers together. The Internet highlights the fact that an innovation which began as an experiment can mature to become part of the infrastructure.

Is there a technology infrastructure within the firm? For most organizations today, the answer to this question is yes. A typical organization has a variety of computers, including mainframes, servers, and desktop personal computers. These machines are often networked together. An employee can connect a computer to this network infrastructure and can access all the functions provided by the company's stock of technology. Some experts also include basic transactions processing applications as a part of the infrastructure, since organizations rely heavily on these systems to conduct business.

Infrastructure begins with the components of information technology, hardware, networks, and software, as the base. A human infrastructure of IT staff members work with these components to create a series of shared technology services. These services change gradually over time and address the key business processes of the firm. Noninfrastructure technology is represented by applications that change frequently to serve new strategies and opportunities (Weill, Broadbent, and Butler 1996).

A National IT Infrastructure

Singapore is a city-state of fewer than three million people occupying a 625-square-kilometer island at the southern end of the Malay Peninsula. A small fishing village at the end of World War II, Singapore has become a developed nation. The country has a literacy rate of almost 90 percent and a life expectancy comparable to other postindustrial countries. Singapore has little in the way of natural resources except for a large, protected harbor and an excellent location along major shipping routes.

The Singapore government first sponsored the development of an EDI capability for expediting the movement of ships through the port. A ship sends cargo manifests in electronic form to freight forwarders in Singapore. Within two hours, the forwarder obtains permits, clears customs, and pays duties for inbound freight. They also obtain export permits for the ship's outbound cargo. As a result the average ship can turn around in 10 hours in Singapore, half the time of most ports (King and Konsynski 1994).

Building on this effort, the National Computer Board in Singapore developed a vision of an "intelligent island." Residents will be able to tap into vast reservoirs of electronic information and services to improve their businesses, to make their working lives easier, and to enhance their personal, social, recreational and leisure options. Text, sound, pictures, video, documents, designs, and other forms of information will be transferred and shared through the high-capacity and high-speed nationwide communications infrastructure made up of fiber optic cables reaching all homes and offices, and a pervasive wireless network operating in tandem.

This information infrastructure will also permeate the physical infrastructure, making mobile telecomputing possible, and making homes, workplaces, and airport, seaport, and surface transportation systems "smarter." A wide range of new infrastructure services, linking government, business, and people, will be created to take advantage of new communications and wireless network technology.

In this vision, some 15 years from now, Singapore will be among the first countries in the world with an advanced nationwide information infrastructure. It will interconnect computers in virtually every home, office, school, and factory. The computer will evolve into an information appliance, combining the functions of the telephone, computer, television, and more. It will provide a wide range of communication means and access to services. The vision, IT2000, is based on the far-reaching use of technology (National Computer Board Web site).

The vehicle for accomplishing this vision of an intelligent island is a fiber optics communications network. Singapore ONE is a national high-capacity network platform that will deliver a potentially unlimited range of multimedia services to the workplace, the home, and the school. It comprises two distinct but interrelated levels—an infrastructure level of networks and switches, and a level of applications and multimedia services. The infrastructure level will consist of a core broadband network connecting several local-access networks. The core, or backbone, of Singapore ONE will be built, owned, and operated by an industry consortium.

Singapore ONE will bring public services closer to the people and make it more convenient for them to carry out government transactions. Examples of services include multifunction kiosks for government transactions and one-stop government centers with video conferencing facilities. High-speed communications will open up a whole new channel for people at home. Potential home applications include high-speed Internet access, entertainment on demand, electronic shopping, home banking, and electronic information services.

Singapore ONE will enable easy access to high-quality multimedia teaching and learning materials and open up new avenues for learning. It will support distance learning and multiparty collaboration by students at different locations. For businesses, a high-speed multimedia network will mean better communication and coordination. An entire marketplace can also make use of new technologies for buying and selling. Potential business applications include video conferencing, multimedia information services for corporations, telecommuting, and electronic commerce (National Computer Board Web site).

The success of the original EDI application, TradeNet, encouraged Singapore to extend its efforts in information technology. TradeNet reengineered the document processing associated with shipping to and from Singapore. The design effort included reducing the number of forms from 20 to 1. TradeNet operates 24 hours a day, and it dramatically reduces the amount of time required to handle the documentation associated with a shipment. A typical turnaround for a document might be 15 minutes with TradeNet; under the old system the same processing could take from one to four days. Freight forwarders also reported cost savings (King and Konsynski 1994). The Singapore Trade Development Board now processes 105,000 documents per staff member each year compared to 27,000 before TradeNet. Processing revenue per staff is Singapore S$465,000 since TradeNet, compared to S$64,000 before the system. From 1986 to 1992 the volume of trade handled by the Trade Development Board more than doubled while the staff decreased in size (Teo, Tan, and Wei 1997).

TradeNet led to a number of other applications. The Port of Singapore Authority installed a system to facilitate the registration of incoming vessels, the deployment of vessels to docks and loading cranes, optimization of loading, and the discharging of vessels ready to leave the port. This system could not have functioned without TradeNet to be sure documentation was ready on time. The success of TradeNet also encouraged Singapore Network Services to develop additional EDI applications, including medicine, business, CAD transmission, real estate, apparel, construction, and general business (Neo, King, and Applegate 1995).

TradeNet began as an effort to reduce the paperwork involved in clearing shipments into and out of Singapore. This system, within a few years, processed the documentation for 95 percent of the air and ship cargo in Singapore. It became a part of the shipping infrastructure for the island. Since it provides technology infrastructure as well, other applications soon appeared. The Singapore Port Authority system is a good example of developing an innovative application because there is an infrastructure to support it.

Did Singapore expect a return on its investment? The government stimulates technology through a series of committees that study specific problems and issue recommendations. The government also provides funding for starting an initiative like TradeNet. Organizationally, Singapore Network Services developed from this effort. Eventually, SNS began to offer other network services throughout Singapore. It is not clear whether it is self-supporting, or whether there is an analysis showing the return to the island of its investment in EDI. At the national level, it is difficult to estimate the payback from investments in infrastructure. However, a variety of organizations involved in trade have clearly benefited from the EDI infrastructure created through TradeNet. IT infrastructure is available; it may well solve some problems on its own, though one of its main roles is to provide the facility for further IT innovations.

A Study of IT Infrastructure in Business

The boundaries of what constitutes IT infrastructure are harder to define in industry. A large-scale study of 25 companies from three industries and four continents tried to define infrastructure and determine how firms view it

(Weill, Broadbent, and Butler 1996). In industry, infrastructure provides a base for future applications more than a solution for immediate problems. In another report on this study, the researchers classified company responses on infrastructure into eight categories (Broadbent et al. 1996):

1. Communications management

2. Applications management

3. Data management

4. Standards management

5. Education management

6. Services management

7. Security

8. IT R&D

They identified five core infrastructure services:

1. Management of corporationwide communication network services

2. Management of groupwide or firmwide messaging services

3. Recommending standards for at least one component of IT architecture (hardware, operating system data, communications, etc.)

4. Security and disaster planning and recovery

5. Technology advice and support services

The study also lists 18 other possible infrastructure services, including the actual management of firmwide applications, databases, consulting services, EDI management, and training, to name a few. What is conspicuously absent from these discussions is the actual hardware, software, and communications environment of the firm. These are definitely components of the organization's technological infrastructure and should be included in any discussion of the topic.

The findings from an analysis of the data in the study are as follows:

1. Firms in different industries have different patterns of IT infrastructure.

2. Firms that need to change products quickly provide more IT infrastructure in general and more infrastructure for applications and data management.

3. Firms with strategies that emphasize business unit synergies have more IT infrastructure.

4. Firms that include IT considerations in the planning process have more IT infrastructure in general.

5. Firms that track the outcome of strategy have more IT infrastructure.

The overall results suggest that infrastructure does provide the firm with opportunities. You need an IT infrastructure in place to meet the competition and respond to changes in the marketplace. A robust infrastructure may play a role in obtaining synergies across business units because the infrastructure promotes coordination and some minimal standards so that SBUs (strategic business units) can interact more easily.

This study did not attempt to measure investment and return from infrastructure, except to report that the typical firm invested 1.7 percent of revenues on the average over five years in firmwide IT infrastructure. This amount was 43 percent of the firm's total IT investment, a substantial percentage. If these numbers can be generalized to other firms, they do not provide much encouragement for demonstrating value from investments in IT. Remember that infrastructure is less likely to solve a current problem than to provide the opportunity to undertake an initiative in the future. *If these numbers are correct, it may be almost impossible to demonstrate a return for over 40 percent of the typical large firm's IT budget that is devoted to infrastructure.*

A National Network Infrastructure

In the 1980s, France developed its Minitel network, one of the first successful mass-market networks. The network is open and decentralized; it is easy for companies to offer services on it. France Telecom gave away a large number of Minitel terminals, established an electronic directory, and stopped distributing printed directories for customers with terminals. Minitel appealed to individuals and to businesses. By the early 1990s, there were over 20,000 service providers on the network. Businesses use the system extensively to provide information to customers and for commerce. This infrastructure investment by the French government through France Telecom was intended to advance technology and business in France. France Telecom today claims that Minitel is profitable, but it is not clear exactly how much has been invested in the network and what return the company has received on that investment.

The Minitel system is a precursor to much that has happened with the Internet. The Net first connected academics and defense contractors; it became essential for exchanging electronic mail, data files, and papers. When the National Science Foundation gradually withdrew its funding from the Internet, it became available for profit-making activities, and business discovered the Internet. The opening of the Internet for profits and the development of the Web and Web browsers account for the phenomenal growth of the Internet.

The Web came into being through frustration: Physicists at the European Laboratory for Particle Physics (CERN) in Europe wanted to post their research results to the Internet to make them available to colleagues. Of course, they wanted colleagues to reciprocate. At that time, finding information posted on the Internet was not easy, and when you did find information it tended to be a linear string of words similar to a research paper.

Tim Berners-Lee, while working at CERN, came up with the idea of a standardized hypertext language to use in navigating the Web. Hypertext is text that is organized with numerous references that take you to other pieces of text or information. If this book were in hypertext, a reference in the body could take you to the complete citation at the end of the chapter. The discussion of a company or a concept in several places in this book could be tied together with links. This effort led to HTML, the Hypertext Markup Language, which has become a standard on the Web. The author of a document inserts special commands into the text; these links connect to other parts of the document, different documents, or even different sites on the Internet.

The next contribution to the Web came from Mark Andreessen, who led a group in creating Mosaic, a graphical browser. Mosaic, followed by Netscape Navigator and Microsoft's Internet Explorer, allows one to follow hypertext links around an Internet Web site or among different sites. Now, by pointing and clicking with a mouse, a user can find information based on links included in documents *without having to know where the link goes, needing an account, or logging on to a computer containing new information.* Soon software vendors developed tools to make it easier to publish material on the Web without having to learn HTML.

We now have an infrastructure that allows for a variety of interesting applications. The basic foundation of the infrastructure is the Internet itself, with all of its communications protocols and thousands of connected computers and communications lines of various capacities. HTML provides another kind of standard that works with the Internet, and a graphical browser lets the user access HTML documents all over the world. Standards make all of this work, just as standards make it possible for telephones to interoperate worldwide.

The Internet represents a major infrastructure that is available to individuals, businesses, and governments around the world. The Department of Defense and the National Science Foundation subsidized the development of this network; currently users of the Net finance it. (The NSF is funding "Internet II," which is to be a very high speed network to experiment with new communications technologies.) I doubt that one could obtain the data, or evaluate the dollar value of the impact of the Net, to do a return-on-investment calculation for this investment. It seems clear that the Internet has provided many different kinds of value to its users, which is what one hopes for in making infrastructure investments.

An Infrastructure Investment That May Demonstrate Immediate Value

The past few years have seen growing interest in corporate Intranets. An Intranet is an internal information system built on the standards of the World Wide Web.

An Intranet looks just like the Internet, but you do not allow access to it by the general public outside the firm. Zona Research estimates that companies invested a little under $3 billion in Intranets in 1996 and that the total could rise to $13 billion by 1999 (*Wall Street Journal* May 13, 1997).

What might you put on an Intranet? At the Stern School of Business at New York University, such a network is under construction. Right now, it contains a class roster of all students, with their social security numbers, names, and e-mail addresses. This Intranet has the ability to download this information into an electronic mail program so that the same message can be sent to the entire class as easily as sending to one person in the class. There is also a page of information, including a photo, for each student in the class to help the faculty get to know students. All of this information is accessible only to the person assigned to teach that class.

For many years, it had been beyond the capabilities of the university to create a foolproof room reservations system. One always had to call two places to reserve a classroom or a conference room, and frequently the rooms were double-booked, leading to much frustration and embarrassment. Now there is a room reservation application on the Stern Intranet. (The various browsers are able to process forms that a user completes to submit to a Web site.) An instructor fills out information about the specific room desired and the event; within a few hours an e-mail message confirms the reservation or suggests another room. Students and faculty are also able to access the course-faculty evaluation forms or "teaching ratings" via the Intranet.

Can a company benefit from this kind of technology investment? Morgan Stanley is a major investment bank, and now a retail broker with its merger with Dean Witter. Morgan Stanley has developed an extensive Intranet containing the research information that various parts of the firm develops. By having it on the Intranet, the information is available to anyone in the company. Members of the firm do not overlook research because it happens to be in someone's bottom desk drawer. (There are various "search engines" on the Web, so that you can search for information on a particular topic.)

At Chrysler, an Intranet has replaced the company telephone directory; it provides a photograph and job descriptions in addition to phone numbers. The automaker expects to use its Intranet to broadcast information around the company, monitor projects, and reduce the amount of time hunting for information. The Chrysler controller collected time sheets from staff to see where they were spending their day. He found that the paperwork to approve equipment purchases was taking up to 18 percent of some employees' time. Now a team is trying to figure out how to streamline the purchasing process using the Intranet. In addition, vehicle program managers post car-design changes to Chrysler's Intranet so that they are instantly available.

The engineering department has invested $750,000 in its part of the Intranet in an effort to link isolated systems. Using the same browser interface, engineers can move from its main software design system, CATIA, to regulatory manuals and home pages that describe how different projects are going. The minivan team home page links to a progress report on the design of a new vehicle's body. Executives can check progress without calling a meeting. The Intranet should help Chrysler achieve its goal of reducing the cycle time for vehicle design to two years from the current four or five years (*Wall Street Journal,* May 13, 1997).

Intranets have the potential to tie together employees in an organization and disparate information systems as well. As vendors create links between Intranet standards and legacy transactions processing systems, it is possible to envision an environment in which the major desktop application for each user is a browser. Using the browser and Intranet, an employee accesses all types of corporate information along with the data from internal, proprietary information systems in the company.

One proprietary study by the consulting firm the Meta Group provides cost studies of investments in Intranets, but it is not possible to verify Meta's calculations from the information they release to the public about their research. Meta claims that 78 percent of the 41 companies in their survey had positive ROIs from Intranets that averaged 38 percent. Some 22 percent of the Intranets studied had negative returns, though these were in the minority. Given all of the creative applications built on top of Intranets, they seem like an excellent example of infrastructure that enables future benefits.

Why Invest in Infrastructure?

I remember an economics professor in graduate school who felt his research demonstrated there was no economic justification for building a transcontinental railroad, at least on the terms the government agreed to with the railroads. A historian might tell us that there were a lot of noneconomic reasons the federal government wanted a railroad that extended from New York to California. The historian's arguments carried the day, but the example does illustrate how hard it can be to justify infrastructure investments.

The major arguments in favor of investing in infrastructure revolve around the need to be ready when an opportunity arises and to have technology up-to-date so you can interoperate with others. Three common rationales for infrastructure investment include the following:

A reduction in the time to market for new products. Otis estimated that it saved four years of development in creating Otisline (see Chapter 5) because it had a flexible database infrastructure in place. Time to market is especially critical in financial services, where custom products appear on very short notice.

Enabling later projects at a lower cost. By having infrastructure in place, possibly charged back to departments, one has only to look at the incremental costs of a new project. It is not necessary to "catch up" on infrastructure to take advantage of a new idea.

Providing flexibility for the unexpected. Managers who use this argument want to have a flexible technology platform ready so that business units can meet new needs faster and for less money than the competition (Weill 1993).

The major difficulty is that you are being asked to invest now for a possible and highly uncertain future benefit. For most of the infrastructure investments described in this chapter, the real benefit of the expenditure comes in the future. Since the role of infrastructure is probably not stressed for projects that build on it, identifying its contribution even in the future will be difficult. Thus, in terms of finding value from IT, it is hard to make the case that you will be able to quantify a significant return from the rather substantial investment firms have to make in IT infrastructure.

It sounds in practice that much of the justification for infrastructure is based on faith. Weill (1993) did find one firm with a creative approach to paying for infrastructure. The company required careful cost/benefit analyses of each project. When a project showed higher than necessary benefits, it was loaded with infrastructure costs to take up the slack. In essence, the company added an "infrastructure tax" to projects, not unlike airline ticket taxes to pay for airports.

What Is an Appropriate IT Infrastructure Today?

The most popular infrastructure today features a client-server architecture and a networked organization. Clients are personal computers with varying amounts of processing power depending on the user's needs. Servers are more powerful computers capable of holding large databases and executing programs faster than clients. Some of these servers will be dedicated to processing transactions like the EDI and JIT applications at Chrysler. A network connects all parts of the organization; it provides for electronic mail and file sharing. The network has a connection to the Internet so that all employees can access this resource. There is an Intranet that is used to reduce paper and as a platform for building applications that become available widely in the organization.

Very few organizations have only the IT infrastructure described earlier. The problem is that information technology has been available since the 1950s; firms have existing applications that do not fit this model. Just as we cannot afford to buy a new car or a new house each year, firms cannot replace all of their applications because technology has moved ahead. While you can buy new and more modern hardware, the problem comes in developing new software or programs to replace old, "legacy" applications. Many of these applications use the programming language COBOL and run on IBM mainframe computers.

One solution to this problem is simply to rename mainframes as large servers, something it appears IBM is trying to accomplish. Another solution is to connect the mainframes to Intranets and other client-server platforms so that they really do look a lot like large servers. This strategy is becoming popular because the cost of mainframes has been falling dramatically, making the decision to convert older systems even more uneconomical.

Whatever your strategy with respect to legacy systems and client server, we are in an era of networking and connectivity. A vital part of a modern infrastructure is client computers for knowledge workers, Internet connections, and the ability to communicate electronically within the organization and with customers and suppliers.

Summary of Results

Infrastructure is vital, but investments in it are hard to justify if you expect an immediate return. Table 6-1 summarizes the investments discussed in this chapter. The Singapore example presents the classic case for infrastructure; a small investment and guidance leads to a facility on which many organizations can build. Networking in Singapore has the potential to transform the nature of commerce on the island and to help achieve the city-state's goals for economic development.

An Intranet may be an infrastructure investment that has the greatest chance of showing a short-term payback. If a company has a great deal of information to communicate, it can probably save some printing, paper, and distribution costs using an Intranet. However, Intranets offer far more. With an infrastructure of servers, networks, and browsers, users can develop many different kinds of applications that are accessible throughout the company. Access to servers can be granted to selected individuals and organizations, for example, customers and suppliers. (Intranets that allow external access are called Extranets.) The real benefits from an Intranet may turn out to be indirect rather than direct.

Infrastructure is something that a firm needs. An investment in infrastructure IT is an investment for the future; it provides the resources needed to take advantage of future opportunities. A substantial portion of a firm's IT budget may be devoted to infrastructure, which means that it will be difficult to show a return on this investment.

Table 6-1

Summary of Infrastructure Investments

Investment	Results	Observations
Singapore networking	Substantial movement of commerce to electronic transactions processing; stimulated "intelligent island" vision	A government-sponsored initiative that was transferred at least partially to the private sector; infrastructure seen as an investment on which to build
Study of 25 companies	Infrastructure provides a base for future applications; can amount to 40 percent+ of IT budget	The return on infrastructure investment is likely to take place in the future
Intranets	Provide an in-house Web site, browsers, and Web infrastructure to encourage users to develop pages and applications	An opportunity to move to a common interface among systems, reduce paper, and increase access to information; very difficult to measure return except for reduced publishing costs

CHAPTER SEVEN

When IT Becomes a Part of Strategy

t is easy to focus on individual IT investments rather than their cumulative impact. Companies budget for individual applications of technology, and the IT staff works on a project basis. For some firms, the combination of all its individual investments in technology far exceeds their individual impact. A good example is the American Hospital Supply, Baxter, Allegiance saga from the Chapter 5. Here, continued investments in technology changed the hospital supply industry and the supply firm's own view of its fundamental business.

There are examples where IT has become intertwined with the basic strategy of the corporation. In these cases, positive experiences with IT investments have provided management with the confidence to incorporate more technology as a part of strategy. The close linking of strategy and technology makes it difficult to measure the return from IT quantitatively, but we may be able to do so qualitatively.

Building a Travel Giant

Rosenbluth Travel, headquartered in Philadelphia, has grown from $40 million in sales in 1980 to $1.3 billion in 1990 (Clemons and Row 1991). It is now one of the five largest travel management companies in the United States and has more than 400 offices.

Rosenbluth was effective in taking advantage of the opportunities offered by deregulation in the travel industry. The firm has used technology to help manage the complexity of modern travel and to obtain economies of scale. Rosenbluth invested in IT over a period of years. While the expenditure in any one year was not inordinate, Rosenbluth created a technology base extremely difficult for a new entrant or even a competitor to match.

Prior to deregulation in 1976, travel agents wrote about 40 percent of all tickets. The role of the agent was only to make a reservation and distribute a ticket. Deregulation changed the role of travel agents, and forced them to manage the increased complexity of travel. American Airline's SABRE system contains 50 million fares and processes millions of changes a month. The airline reservation systems used by travel agents were biased toward the airlines, though no more so than one would find calling the airline itself for information. The travel agent, however, could be expected to help the client without a bias toward a particular airline. By 1985 travel agencies were distributing more than 80 percent of air tickets.

Businesses are very interested in managing their travel. It is the third largest expense for most services firms after payroll and information technology. Firms began to negotiate rates with airlines, hotels, and rental-car companies. One of Rosenbluth's major business focuses has been the corporate travel market.

The following list of critical technology moves by Rosenbluth illustrates how the firm has used IT for expanding its business:

- About 1981 the firm experimented with processing data from airline computerized reservation systems (CRSs) to provide information for corporate accounts.

- In 1983 Rosenbluth introduced a product called READOUT that listed flights by fare instead of by time of departure. This program made it possible to see the fare implications of taking a particular flight. The normal flight display was by departure time, and the agent had to move to another screen to obtain fare information.

- In 1986 a proprietary back-office system, VISION, created a highly flexible reporting system for clients. The system created a record of transactions made for a client at the time of ticketing no matter the location of the agency or the CRS in use. This system gave Rosenbluth independence from the data provided by the airline CRS. During 1986 Rosenbluth estimated that it invested nearly half of its pretax profit in the system. The VISION system was more flexible and produced reports about two months earlier than agencies using only the airline CRS. Rosenbluth used VISION to negotiate special fares with the airlines on heavily traveled routes the system identified.

Instead of competing for corporate clients by offering to rebate part of its commissions, Rosenbluth tried to create a cooperative relationship with clients.

It promised clients to reduce overall travel costs through lower fares and used VISION reports to document the savings.

- In 1988 Rosenbluth used a new feature in United's Apollo reservation system to support intelligent workstations. The new Rosenbluth system, PRECISION, made client and individual employee travel profiles, and the READOUT database of flights listed by increasing fares, available to the agent making a reservation. ULTRAVISION is another system that runs with the normal reservation process, monitoring transactions for accuracy and completeness.

- During 1990-1991, Rosenbluth began installing USERVISION in its offices. This system lets the user make flexible queries about corporate travel. The data are one day old compared to the 45-day lag typical of the airline CRS data.

These initiatives reflect a tremendous growth period, as Rosenbluth's sales increased from $400 million in 1987 to $1.3 billion in 1990, while the number of offices increased from 85 to over 400.

The firm has been extremely successful. Business and technology strategy were developed together in an integrated approach to growth. The firm took risks in developing new uses of IT and the in-house expertise to implement systems successfully. Rosenbluth's technology strategy competes through value-added services rather than being the low-cost producer through rebates. It also took advantage of technology to market new services to its clients. The company meets jointly with its clients and service providers to help the client negotiate the lowest possible fares.

It is interesting to note the role of infrastructure in Rosenbluth's strategy. The company built on an infrastructure supplied by the major airline CRS vendors. The investments by the airlines made it possible for Rosenbluth to offer custom programs and new services to its clients. The travel company benefited greatly from an infrastructure created by others.

French Office Supplies and IT

Even a relatively small company can invest in information technology to gain a competitive advantage. Brun Passot is one of four major competitors in the French office supplies industry; however, these companies have a combined market share of only 25 percent. There are some 5,000 office products distributors in France! The fall of trade barriers among European Community nations has meant that French suppliers now have to compete with British, German, and even U.S. firms (Jelassi and Figon 1994).

Brun Passot was started as a family firm in 1949. By the early 1990s with 160 employees it offered 12,000 products to 6,000 customers, delivering to up to 15,000 locations. From 1970 to 1992 its sales rose from 15 million to 254 million French francs (FF). In 1980 Brun Passot decided that it could distinguish itself from competitors by offering customers the opportunity to purchase items electronically. By 1983 the company developed Bureautel, a system that ran on Minitel, the French national videotext network, which allowed customers to place orders electronically. Brun Passot's own employees could also inquire against its inventory and obtain sales and cash-flow information from the system.

In 1989 the company enhanced this system by issuing a credit card with a predefined maximum purchase limit per customer department. As the customer placed orders, their value was subtracted from the credit card. The card was not actually used for payment, but as a way to let customer personnel order supplies without generating a purchase order or getting management approval. The system made it easier to order from Brun Passot. The card also helped customers maintain control over their department budgets for office supplies.

By 1985 large customers encouraged Brun Passot to develop a PC-based system for them. This system was less expensive for customers than Minitel; they could centralize ordering even though requests were generated from multiple locations. As the capacity of the French telephone system grew, this system was expanded to provide color photos of each of Brun Passot's 12,000 products. In 1989 Brun Passot developed the capability to electronically send product files, delivery status reports, purchase quotes, shipping notices, invoices, payments, and e-mail messages to clients. (Unfortunately, the company had to print paper invoices, too, since the French justice system did not recognize electronic invoices.)

Brun Passot estimates its investment in these applications at FF550,000 with ongoing operating costs of about FF100,000 covered by fees paid by users. By 1992, 40 percent of Brun Passot's orders were electronic. Before the end of the decade, the company expects the number of non-Minitel electronic orders to double. The introduction of these systems simplified procedures and freed 25 people to do more selling and visit customers. Since it is easier to predict customer demand, stock turnover has risen from 9 to 16 times a year; inventory management costs have also dropped 7 percent (Jelassi and Figon 1994).

Brun Passot realized as it faced increasing competition, technology might help it differentiate its services from others in this crowded industry. It successfully managed the development of multiple applications of technology. Management had to do more than just create systems. It changed the way the firm operated to take advantage of the capabilities provided by electronic links to customers. Brun Passot recognized that a computer is more than a computational device; modern information technology provides new opportunities through communications. As technology contributed more and more to the firm, management began to see electronic commerce as a part of Brun Passot's strategy: Information technology and strategy became intertwined.

In the case of Brun Passot again we see a company taking advantage of infrastructure. Its first applications were on the Minitel system, a low-speed graphics network developed by France Telecom. This infrastructure features easy program development and, because of its success, a large number of Minitel terminals throughout France so that it was likely a customer had access to the system. With a network and terminal infrastructure in place, Brun Passot had only to develop its order entry application.

Is State Street a Bank?

State Street Bank in Boston has made major investments in information technology. Its mission statement, in part, reads: "State Street combines information technology with banking, trust, investment, and securities processing capabilities to support the investment strategies of our customers worldwide" (Francalanci 1995). State Street provides services primarily to institutional investors with a focus on servicing and managing financial assets, and on commercial lending. In 1996 some 64 percent of its operating profits came from financial asset services, 21 percent from commercial lending, and 15 percent from investment management. State Street is the leading mutual fund custodian in the United States, servicing 2,729 registered funds for a 39 percent market share. In addition to service, the bank provides accounting and daily pricing, fund administration, accounting for different classes of shares, off-shore funds, and shareholder accounting. The bank has viewed information technology as a major component of its strategy. It spends up to 10 percent of revenue on technology.

The bank targets a number of categories of clients:

Investment companies and managers

Large corporations

Medium and small companies

Individuals

Government organizations

Insurance companies

Unions

Nonprofit organizations.

For 20 years, the bank has developed IT applications to meet the increasingly demanding needs of its customers and to be a leader in its field. From batch processing, the bank moved toward on-line accounting systems and applications that could handle multiple currencies. In the 1990s it implemented applications to give its customers direct access to nearly real-time data on funds through Windows-based PCs.

The bank's objective in developing this application was to reduce the amount of time an investment manager spends gathering information (by some estimates 80 percent of the day) so the manager can spend more time deciding on the right investment. The bank realized the data it provided had to be up-to-date, and that it needed to provide customers with a friendly interface to its systems.

Has the bank been successful? Since the early 1980s the bank's return on equity has averaged 17 percent or better, hitting 18.1 percent in 1996. Between 1988 and 1993, the compound growth rates of fee revenue was 16 percent, while total revenue and net income grew at 14 percent management (Francalanci 1995). At the end of 1997, State Street had custody of $3 trillion and $300 billion of assets under management.

Some analysts believe that State Street looks more like a service company than a bank! The bank was successful in providing investment management and processing services, encouraging it to continue investing in IT. Its strategy became dependent upon technology to deliver products and services. As the bank proved it could be successful in converting its investment into applications, it incorporated more IT into its strategy. Today, the bank is unique among banks as an information processor and fund manager.

EDI as a Part of Strategy

The H. E. Butt Grocery company is the thirteenth largest grocery retailer in the United States with sales over $3 billion. The company operates over 200 full-service supermarkets in Texas. The long-term strategy of the company had always been to compete on low prices. The company pursued low prices through continuous cost reductions.

Technology became a major factor in HEB's strategy when it started to implement point-of-sales scanner systems in its retail stores in the 1970s. By 1990 e-mail was a major part of operations and accounted for a significant percentage of data communications. Also in the early 1990s HEB installed mini-computers in all stores linked to headquarters. This link was used for the ongoing exchange of data on sales, orders, and personnel. The firm eventually established a VSAT satellite system linking all stores and headquarters.

When Wal-Mart began to offer grocery products at lower prices than the typical supermarket, HEB wanted to try the same kind of relationship this discounter had with its suppliers. Butt's first experiment was with Proctor & Gamble. The idea behind the "continuous replenishment" program (CRP) was that P&G would accept electronic data from HEB's warehouse, determine the order quantity needed, assemble the delivery, and notify HEB electronically that a shipment was on the way. P&G received daily demand data electronically from the stores along with inventory position from the warehouses.

This coupling of order processing eliminated between 6 and 10 days from the order cycle. Warehouse stockout levels fell from 6 percent to 1 percent for CRP products. HEB felt the CRP program resulted in a reduction in inventory levels and reduced ordering costs for its warehouses. This success with P&G encouraged the company to set up CRP relationships with other vendors. The key, of course, to making CRP work is electronic data interchange. In eight months, Butt went from 10 to 500 partners communicating with it using EDI. By mid-1994, 96 percent of HEB's grocery orders came from EDI or a combination of EDI and CRP.

The next step after CRP is efficient consumer response, or ECR. This program consists of a number of components; its objective is to drive more slack from the order cycle while maintaining customer service levels. The first part of the program involves ordering directly from POS (point of sale) data from the stores, something that requires very accurate scanning. With this information, the entire supply chain could change. Some products could go directly to the store, bypassing the warehouse. At the warehouse, complete information would allow for "cross docking," where goods arrive on an incoming dock and are immediately shipped from an outgoing dock without ever being placed on the warehouse shelves. If successful, warehouses would shrink dramatically and become distribution centers. Much more responsibility would be delegated to the store manager to review POS data and to verify computer-generated orders.

Information technology at H. E. Butt probably has had a direct return. The company makes one believe that it carefully cost justifies investments in IT before proceeding. Its main criterion for approval is the ability of the investment to drive cost from the system so Butt can continue to compete on low prices. Beyond the probable cost savings, however, HEB's investments in IT have made technology an integral part of its strategy.

IT As a Competitive Necessity

One way to interest a manager in a new innovation is to show that a competitor is planning to adopt this innovation. Companies do respond to competition to avoid being put at a disadvantage. Banks provide a good example of investing in technology for competitive reasons. In an early study of ATM deployment, Banker and Kauffman (1988) found that ATM adoption provided a limited advantage to certain banks. They collected data on the characteristics of a number of Pennsylvania commercial and mutual savings banks to assess the impact of ATM deployment. The researchers constructed a model that predicted the bank's market share of demand and savings deposits. The study used the type of institution, physical characteristics of a branch, other branch characteristics, the presence of an ATM at a branch, and whether or not the ATM was part of the dominant network in the area, to predict deposits.

The model estimated market shares for both demand (checking) and savings deposits; the researchers used a number of different partitions of the data to understand the impact of ATM deployment. The single most interesting finding was that membership in the dominant ATM network had a positive association with the branch's market share of local deposits. Customers evidently benefit from having a large number of networked ATMs from which to choose, so they gravitate toward a bank with network connections. The presence of a local ATM had no correlation with market share. When the study examined center city Philadelphia alone, it showed that network membership was not associated with market share. Since the center city is dominated by commercial banks, this finding seemed reasonable.

Network membership was not significantly associated with deposit market share in the area where the network was concentrated. In the branches where the network was not dominant, network membership was strongly associated with deposit market share. These results suggest that network membership is more important than the presence of an ATM. The ATM, at the time of this study, replaced a teller in an existing branch. Network membership meant that a customer could obtain access to his or her bank from multiple locations; you did not have to be at your own bank's branch to do business.

In a more recent study, Dos Santos and Peffers (1995) examined the impact of ATM deployment in 3,838 U.S. banks during the 1979-1983 time period. They collected data on the year in which the bank adopted ATMs from 1971 through 1979. The model predicts market share during 1979-1983, normalized by 1972 market share, for personal loans. It also predicts the change in net income compared to income for 1972 divided by total bank assets. (It is difficult to see a link between ATMs and personal loans, but personal loans are highly correlated with demand deposits, and thus serve as a surrogate variable.) The model controls for growth, cost containment strategy, retail focus, and bank structure and size. It also includes variables for whether statewide branching and statewide ATM placement is allowed, and whether the state mandates shared ATMs.

The results show that early adopters of ATMs in the 1971-1973 period were associated with higher market shares from 1979 to 1983, and this advantage was sustained through 1983. However, for banks adopting ATMs after 1973, there were few significant findings. The variance explained by the models is rather low, however, with a maximum of a little less than 15 percent. When the researchers applied their model to predicting the change in operating income since 1972 per $100 of bank assets, they found that ATM adoption was generally significantly associated with positive changes in operating income, though the benefits appeared greatest for the earliest adopters. Here the model explained up to 42 percent of the variance in performance.

Dos Santos and Peffers (1995) feel that their results demonstrate an association between being a first mover in adopting ATMs and both market share and income. While studies like this cannot prove causality, the fact that adoption in an early period is associated with performance in a later period does eliminate one interpretation: 1979-1983 performance could not cause 1972 adoption! However, there could be other variables responsible for both adoption in the early 1970s and bank performance in the early 1980s. For example, aggressive and innovative management might be the first to invest in ATMs and the first to understand how to improve market share and performance regardless of technology.

Dos Santos and Peffers noted that it took banks considerable time to learn how to best utilize ATMs. Some banks had to revise and improve their back-office transactions processing systems to function with ATMs. Banks had to experiment with where to place ATMs and had to consider security concerns in their placement as well. Banks also had to provide a mix of human tellers and ATMs, delaying some of the benefits from adoption.

The findings from both ATM studies, then, suggest an early advantage from installing ATMs and joining a large network. How long could a bank sustain that advantage? The second study suggests that there may be lasting benefits from being an early adopter, though the mechanism for maintaining such an advantage is not clear. Now virtually all banks have ATMs and are members of one or more networks. Customers clearly like ATMs and network connections; there is very little reason for a bank not to join an ATM network. In fact, because competitors offer ATMs and are in networks, a new bank is almost forced to invest in this technology. Certainly by the 1990s ATMs are a *competitive necessity* for banking.

Given that one has to provide ATMs, banks have realized various benefits from this technology. They have installed ATMs in nonbank locations such as supermarkets, where opening a branch with a complete staff might not be attractive. Some banks are closing expensive branches and installing ATMs instead. However, since all banks can follow this strategy, it is unlikely one will gain a significant advantage from it.

The airline industry offers another example of IT as a competitive necessity. To start an airline today, you would have to invest in some kind of technology for making a reservation. The traveling public has become accustomed to being able to make reservations and obtain tickets easily, either physical or electronic.

Southwest Airlines, based in Phoenix, has been in business for 25 years and is the fifth largest U.S. airline. It has over 2,000 flights per day and carries more than 45 million passengers a year. For a number of years, Southwest was very successful as an airline while refusing to pay ticketing fees to airline CRSs. Competition, combined with the attractiveness of the World Wide Web infrastructure, has forced Southwest to extend its reservations system.

The company has its own mainframe reservations system and operates 10 call centers to take reservations; the reservations end of the business employs several thousand people. Southwest has constructed a Web site, called Home Gate, which connects to its existing reservations computer. A traveler accesses the site with a browser, chooses a destination, travel date, and flight, and provides a credit card number to pay for the travel. He or she receives a ticket confirmation number and itinerary that they can use for airport check-in (*Internet*, May 1997).

Southwest believes this Web site will save money because it can take some of the load off the call centers. However, even if there is no direct return, Southwest had little choice but to develop its Web site. Customers can use one of several Web systems to book flights on any carrier that is willing to pay booking fees. Southwest needs a presence on the Web as well to remain competitive.

Barnes & Noble, the largest U.S. book retailer, has established a subsidiary named BarnesandNoble.com to sell books on the World Wide Web. The site features personalized book recommendations based on a user's profile, chats with authors, book groups, reviews, and bulletin boards. While this site sounds attractive and may generate business, Barnes & Noble was forced to create it because of Amazon Books, a company that has been extremely successful selling books over the WWW. Barnes & Noble is almost two years behind Amazon Books in getting its Web site up and running (*ComputerWorld*, June 16,1997). Will the two companies fight for a fixed market, or will the convenience and services they offer increase the market for books bought on-line? Will the benefits of having two large on-line book retailers accrue to the companies, or primarily to their customers?

Competitive Advantage to the Customer

Investments for strategy and to meet a competitive challenge may not actually benefit the company making them. A firm may be forced, as in the examples mentioned earlier, to adopt new technology to stay even with the competition. In this case, it is not so much return on investment in IT, but rather what is the cost of *not* investing? Will a firm lose customers and market share because it does not have a particular technology in place? Can you enter a new line of business without investing in the technology that competitors have adopted? What kinds of services do customers expect?

Information technology has been an important part of Federal Express's strategy; its chief information officer has said that "in an era of just-in-time delivery—in which a company may keep inventory on hand for as little as a few hours—information about the location and status of freight has become just as critical to customers as receiving the box intact" (*Wall Street Journal,* June 2, 1997). Technology has become a part of the competition among carriers; UPS and FedEx spend about $1 billion a year on IT, whereas DHL in Brussels is investing $1.5 billion in technology over five years. UPS is trying to catch up with FedEx on customer service; it is offering direct mainframe connections to large customers, giving away thousands of computers and tracking software to other companies, and even renting a UPS phone to smaller shippers. While the express companies battle for market share, customers have benefited tremendously.

Technology that becomes a necessity may not create much benefit for the firm that invests in it, except that the technology allows the firm to continue in a line of business. Who does benefit from investments of this type? The cynical answer might be the vendors of various kinds of technology. However, a better response is that *customers* benefit from better quality goods and services, and especially better customer service.

Customers are much better off from the presence of ATMs. An ATM is convenient and allows one to access cash without presenting a check at his or her own bank. With an ATM, you do not have to worry about a foreign bank accepting your check; from ATMs around the world you can withdraw cash. While airlines have certainly benefited from computerized reservations systems, so have customers. You can use a CRS to compare flights, times, ticket prices, and even on-time statistics for each flight. A consumer can make a reservation on a flight and complete the transaction over the telephone or the Internet.

Economists talk about a concept called "consumer surplus."

Figure 7-1 shows the demand and supply curves for quantities of specially engraved promotional pens. The market price for the pens is $15, and the total number sold at this price will be quantity Q. This result comes from the intersection of the demand and supply curves. Consumer Z is willing to pay $15 and receives no "surplus." Consumer X is the best off; he is willing to pay $20, but only has to spend $15. His surplus is $5. Consumer Y is willing to pay $16, but only has to pay $15, so she has a consumer surplus of $1. The surplus for all consumers is represented by the area in the triangle ABD. There is also a producer surplus represented by the area in the triangle BCD.

In an interesting study, Brynjolfsson (1996) examined the consumer surplus that has resulted from declining prices in the sales of computer and related equipment, excluding software. His estimate is that consumers keep about three out of every four dollars of gross value created by computers.

Figure 7-1

Consumer Surplus

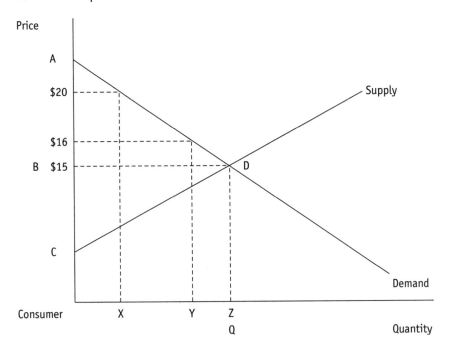

How does consumer surplus relate to investments in strategic and competitive information technology? From a theoretical standpoint, consumer surplus increases as prices drop. In Figure 7-1, the supply curve shifts down when companies are willing to supply more pens at each price; the shift makes the consumer surplus triangle ABD larger. The competitive use of IT reduces costs and prices through applications like those at H. E. Butt. Wal-Mart and others stimulated this grocery firm to invest in IT so that it could continue to be a low-price store. The competitive use of technology has, in many instances, reduced prices (or held down price increases), which contributes directly to consumer surplus.

In addition, customers have come to expect ATMs, airline CRSs, financial accounts that sweep cash into investment funds automatically, and many other services. Technological competition may not always create an economic consumer surplus, but it does provide benefits in the form of service and convenience. A bank ATM can save time for the customer, something the customer may be able to value from a dollar standpoint. FedEx's Web site for tracking a package saves time on the telephone. The fact that UPS had a similar site within a month means that FedEx was not able to get a sustainable advantage from its investment. Neither carrier was able to raise its prices directly to pay for their Web services, so the benefits from their investments in technology all went to the customer.

Of course, it is not always the case that the consumer is the only winner from strategic investments in IT. We have seen that the airline CRS vendors gained significant direct and indirect revenue from deploying their systems to travel agents. It is also possible that a strategic application can result in greater sales for an entire industry. It will be interesting to see if electronic commerce on the Internet increases sales for the industries that participate in it by making it easier for consumers to order their products.

Summary of Results

In this chapter we have reviewed investments in IT for strategic and competitive reasons, as summarized in Table 7-1. In several of the examples of strategic investment—Rosenbluth Travel, Braun Passot, State Street Bank, and H. E. Butt—there is evidence of payoff from the investment. However, the data needed are not available to calculate a return. Since the technology interacted with strategy and was instrumental in changing each company's approach to business, it would be very hard to calculate a return even with access to the numbers. The qualitative evidence is very persuasive, though it should be remembered that the IT investment was a part of an entire management strategy. The benefits described for these firms did not come from IT alone.

This chapter also explored the case of purely competitive systems, investments in technology undertaken to respond to competitors. It is unlikely that UPS worried about the cost of providing a package-tracking ability on its Web site; FedEx already had a site and that was reason enough to invest. Because it is so difficult to protect technological innovations that rely on software or the Internet, such applications can be copied easily by competitors. Innovations quickly become expected features as competitors rush to imitate the first mover.

The real benefits of investments in strategic and competitive IT may, in fact, go to the consumer in the form of an economic or service surplus. If you cannot raise prices to recover the investment or generate revenue from it in some way, the customer is likely to capture the benefits. Society, at least con-

Table 7-1

Summary of Strategic IT Investments

Investment	Results	Observations
Rosenbluth Travel	Invested up to half of pretax profits in IT; became a key in growth strategy	Built on airline CRS infrastructure to offer better products to clients
Braun Passot	Began with Minitel and grew to PC applications	Built on existing infrastructure; IT demonstrated value, and management built more of its strategy around it
State Street Bank	Emphasized financial services for funds; IT enabled it to capture significant market share	Technology became a part of strategy as it proved successful in serving clients
H. E. Butt	History of IT investment to reduce costs and focus on low-price strategy	EDI, CRP, ECR all contribute to lower costs; the total IT investment has become a part of HEB's strategy to compete
ATM studies	1. There was little advantage from ATMs except where the bank belonged to the major ATM network 2. First movers appeared to obtain and sustain an advantage in market share and income	ATMs are a necessity, especially membership in a network
Southwest Airlines CRS	A Web interface for making reservations; a necessity for competition	Southwest will not pay booking fees to CRS vendors, so it must find alternative channels to make a reservation
UPS, FedEx	IT as a strategy becomes a basis for competition	Customers benefit as business is redefined from packages to packages plus information about them

sumers, are better off, though it is not at all clear the supplier has obtained a return from its investment in IT. When a firm is forced to invest in IT to remain competitive without much likelihood of increased profits or market share, the main benefit may be that the firm remains in business and avoids losing market share.

CHAPTER EIGHT

Investing in IT to Enable Change

Management may invest in IT to change a process, or to change the entire organization. Some changes happen by accident, whereas in other instances they are planned. Planned changes may affect just one work group, for example, a department adopts a project management package or decides to use groupware to coordinate its activities. In other instances, the technology has an impact on the structure and operations of the organization as a whole. In this chapter, we look at examples of investments in technology that are associated with major structural changes in organizations.

The T-Form Organization

In my book *The T-Form Organization* (1996) I wrote about a new form of technology-enabled organization called the T-Form. What are the characteristics of this new type of technology-based corporation? The manager who designs an organization has a great deal of freedom in choosing its structure. *Given the objective that most firms have today of being highly efficient and minimizing overhead, most managers will employ technology to produce the kind of organization described in Figure 8-1.*

The T-Form organization has a flat structure, a structure that has a minimum number of layers of management. The classical approach to organization design stresses concepts like the span of control. How many subordinates can a supervisor manage? Numbers like seven or eight are popular answers to this question.

Other designers say, "When a person has too much work to do, we provide him or her with subordinates to help out."

Figure 8-1

The T-Form Organization

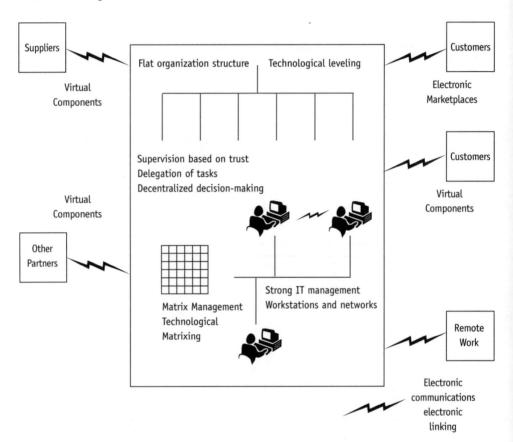

Having a rigid span of control and providing subordinates whenever needed is a very expensive way to design organizations. Over the years, firms have built up huge bureaucracies that are very costly to support. The T-Form organization substitutes technology for layers of management. First, communications technology demolishes old ideas of spans of control; a manager can stay in contact with and "supervise" a large number of subordinates electronically. Of course, this supervision will be more remote and will require much more trust than the close supervision made possible by sitting near one's subordinates.

Second, technology will be used to help the manager perform his or her tasks rather than hiring a subordinate. The kinds of support available through a personal computer workstation connected to a network makes a manager far more productive today than in the past.

Another objective for the T-Form corporation is to remain flexible. Market needs and business conditions change rapidly. The firm will have to respond quickly to these changes, a characteristic not associated with large bureaucracies. The T-Form organization uses matrix management and temporary work groups to create this flexibility. Matrix management involves multiple assignments for staff members. The information technology function has used this structure for many years; systems analysts and programmers typically work on more than one project at a time. They report to a project manager for each project, and to an overall manager of systems and programming.

Matrix management was popular 20 years ago, but seems to have fallen out of favor, except in naturally team-oriented activities like systems development. One reason may be that matrix management is more complex than the typical hierarchical form of organization; it also can be unsettling to employees who have multiple reporting relationships. Electronic communications, however, make it easier to form task forces of employees who cut across a number of functional areas of the business. In fact, it is likely that these task forces will include individuals from external organizations. The engineer designing a new automobile will include personnel on the design team from outside parts suppliers.

Technology alone is not enough to produce the T-Form organization; to take advantage of IT, the culture and climate of the organization have to change. In addition to matrices and temporary task forces, management has to decentralize decision making. In order to provide flexibility, firms have found that managers closest to a problem are in the best position to solve it. Technology makes it possible to provide managers at any level in the firm with information; management has to be willing to delegate decision making to individuals who are close to a problem.

What does delegating decision making mean? You have the ability to make a decision if you can commit the organization and/or its resources *without prior approval.* You may have to report on your actions, but you will only rarely be overruled, and you are free to act without checking with someone else first.

Decentralized decision making implies that there is a high level of trust in the organization. Management must have faith in managers at all levels in the firm, and they must believe that the information systems in place provide the appropriate information for managers to take action. Trust, then, is an essential part of the culture in a T-Form organization.

The T-Form organization is much less concerned with the physical structure of the firm; instead it is interested in a "logical view." What you see may not be exactly what is there! We are used to organizations that are housed in an identifiable location; these firms have well-defined organization charts that show where everyone reports. The T-Form organization uses communications technology like electronic mail, groupware, and distributed offices to provide itself and its employees with more flexibility. Reporting relationships can and will change as the firm faces new demands.

One of the major business and technology trends in the last part of the twentieth century has been the development of interorganizational systems (IOS). Companies have established electronic links with their customers and suppliers. Beginning in the late 1960s with the American Hospital Supply order entry system, firms have been forging links with the organizations with whom they do business.

At first, these links focused on routine, well-specified transactions. Electronic data interchange (EDI) has proven very effective in a variety of industries, including trucking, auto manufacturing, and retailing, among others. In addition to routine transactions, firms can easily establish electronic mail and groupware connectivity with external organizations. Manufacturing firms are working more closely with suppliers; electronic communications facilitate this kind of relationship.

Reengineering focuses our attention on business processes regardless of the department or functions that might have partial responsibility for a task. An order entry system cuts across a number of departments from order taking to inventory control to the warehouse. Instead of looking at each of these functions, process engineering concentrates on the order cycle process itself. In the T-Form organization, functional organization is less important than today; this kind of firm identifies its processes and has process "owners" who are responsible for seeing that the process works.

The T-Form organization has a number of *virtual components*. A virtual component is a part of a company that exists physically in a traditional organization, but that has been replaced by an electronic version. Where did the inventory at Chrysler go when the company implemented EDI and JIT manufacturing? It exists in a different form through information systems that let Chrysler's suppliers know exactly what to produce and when to deliver it to a Chrysler plant.

Allegiance offers a stockless service to hospitals; it delivers medical supplies to the department that needs them on a just-in-time basis. The hospital has a virtual inventory that is kept and supplied by Allegiance. Virtual components are an important part of the T-Form organization; they are responsible for much of its efficiency and flexibility.

A virtual organization can be created through a negotiated agreement with another firm. You could say that the Allegiance stockless inventory service involves a negotiated agreement with each customer. Later in this chapter we look at Calyx and Corolla, a direct-sales flower company. This firm has negotiated agreements with growers to supply flower arrangements and with Federal Express to provide delivery services.

One could argue that these types of agreements represent a new form of *strategic alliance* with other corporations. These companies have intertwined their production, logistics, and even their marketing functions to create what looks like a traditional organization to the customer. Note that an alliance implies more than just a "make or buy" decision; the firm is purchasing more than a component to plug into some part of the organization. An alliance involves a pooling of interests, not a onetime purchase or sale. The firms in an alliance become interdependent and form a partnership; each is interested in the success of the other.

An alliance lets each firm do what it does best; that is, each firm operates where it has a comparative advantage. A trend in today's business is to return to one's "core competence" after many companies diversified or bought other firms. Xerox has sold its financial services divisions to concentrate on being a document processing company. It would not make much sense for Federal Express to acquire firms in order to ship their products; FedEx's core competence is in running a first-class delivery and transportation system. It can be a strategic partner with a number of businesses.

Investments in information technology enable the T-Form organization. Each of these investments may show a return, but it is their combined effect that is of most interest. All of the technology taken together creates a firm whose structure and operations differ from the traditionally organized enterprise. The T-Form organization is more flexible, responsive, and efficient than the comparable hierarchical firm. Can we show a return from the T-Form organization's investment in IT based on structure and operations? While I would like the answer to this question to be yes, I have doubts that anyone will be able to tie technology to structure to the performance of the entire organization. The rest of this chapter presents examples of firms with structures partially enabled by technology. For the most part, these firms are successful. However, it would be very difficult to claim that technology investments are entirely responsible for this success. The technology does appear to make a significant contribution to these organizations, a contribution that is very hard to measure in a conventional return-on-investment framework.

The Frito-Lay Hybrid Organization

Frito-Lay is one of the leading snack food companies in the United States. Management made a major decision in the early 1980s to invest $40 million in a risky new project to develop hand-held computers for the route sales force. Frito-Lay had about 10,000 routes at that time; each sales representative called on a number of customers. Before the hand-held computer, the job involved a lot of paperwork; drivers had to reconcile their cash accounts at home in the evening, and there were frequent disputes with the company.

The project was justified primarily on the belief that it would increase efficiency and provide more time for the route sales force to actually sell the product. It should also reduce "stales," merchandise that had to be discarded because it had not sold before losing its freshness.

The hand-held computer was specially designed for Frito-Lay; there was no suitable device on the market at that time. The company also had to develop a satellite-based, nationwide communications network to move the data from the sales office to headquarters in Dallas. A large number of mainframe computer programs were modified, and computers were installed at the distribution centers to upload the data from the drivers to corporate computers in Plano, Texas. The mainframe also downloads price changes and promotions to the hand-held computers. On Monday, it sends each sales representative a review of the last week's result for their routes.

The hand-held computer allows the sales representative to scroll through the products that an account might order and indicate the quantities delivered. For the first time, Frito-Lay obtained data on exactly what its cash accounts were ordering; the accuracy of the records and the accounting functions meant that drivers did not have to spend hours reconciling receipts from the cash accounts. The system also reduced the need to take physical inventories and freed time for the drivers to provide better customer service.

The hand-held computer improved operations at Frito-Lay; it also provided detailed information that had not been available before for cash accounts. With checkout scanners, grocery stores were developing better information on sales than manufacturers. The data collected by the drivers with their hand-held computers helped to give Frito-Lay comparable information.

Frito-Lay developed a series of computer applications, called an Executive Information System, to facilitate management inquiries about sales. Given the new information, Frito-Lay management began a series of steps to change the way in which it handled marketing; the concept was one of micromarketing. The company made the data from the hand-held computer available in a large database; regional sales managers could make queries that told them in great detail what products were selling at what stores. A manager could find out the answer to the question "How many bags of Fritos were sold at the 7-11 on Morris Avenue in Summit, N.J., last week?"

Each of the 32 divisional sales managers for Frito-Lay can get reports on individual accounts for each brand and package size by type of store. The manager can see pricing moves by competitors.

With this kind of information available, Frito-Lay no longer has to depend on national advertising campaigns; it can target advertising to the local market and anticipate its effects. The collection of detailed data on sales and the availability of the data in a database enabled this new marketing strategy. Frito-Lay laid off 1,800 employees in 1991, with 1,000 of these individuals coming from the headquarters staff. We suspect many of these employees were middle-level managers; there is less for the middle to do, since data are made available to lower levels of management and to senior levels. What role is left for managers who used to gather and summarize data for different levels of management?

Frito-Lay is a good example of a strategy changing the way the organization is structured and how it operates. The strategy was enabled by IT, and then the technology supported changes in structure. Decision-making power moved upward to senior management and downward to division managers, allowing a redefinition and reduction in the role of middle managers.

Different Structures at Mrs. Fields Cookies

Mrs. Fields Cookies is an oft-cited example of a firm that has used information technology as a part of its organization structure. Mrs. Fields Cookies is a chain of small retail outlets, typically found in shopping malls, which sell several varieties of cookies and a few other selected food items. In 1988 there were approximately 500 retail stores worldwide. Stores follow a consistent formula of uniform quality and price regardless of location. However, Mrs. Fields Cookies has a unique structure; it has two parallel organizations, one that has a traditional span of control and another that has a very high span of control.

The traditional hierarchy is formed by 500 store managers, 105 district sales managers, 17 regional directors, 4 senior regional directors, a vice president of operations, and finally Debbie Fields. The span of control of this hierarchy is about 1:5.

The second organization is a formal reporting relationship for control purposes; here 500 store managers report to 6 store controllers, who report to the vice president of operations. The span of control between store managers and controllers is 35 to 75:1, which represents a very flat organization structure. The "human" side of management at Mrs. Fields is through a traditional hierarchy; the "numbers" side is a flat organization made possible through information technology.

Until recently, every shop was wholly owned by the company rather than franchised, and the company was under the strong centralized control of Mrs. Fields and her husband. The unique organization of Mrs. Fields Cookies allowed the owners maximum flexibility in adapting its offerings to the changing tastes of customers in a "fad" business.

IT is an integral part of the structure of Mrs. Fields Cookies. Each store is connected on-line to a central database, and there is extensive automation of production quotas, sales volumes, and other functions based on recent daily sales records for each store. In fact, each store is given hourly sales projections and reports hourly sales results. All ordering of supplies (e.g., chocolate chips) is done automatically from the central database with direct delivery to the store.

Each store's product mix, sales quotas, and special promotions are customized by an expert system that adapts to hourly sales. The company also uses IT for coordination, through voice mail and electronic mail, so that each store manager has direct personal interaction with Mrs. Fields herself. Companywide announcements are frequently broadcast to each store by voice mail, significantly personalizing the announcement compared to memos and reports. (Debbie Fields was a cheerleader in high school, and voice mail seems a natural way to rally the troops.) Each manager may send Mrs. Fields electronic messages for particular problems and expect a personal response within 48 hours.

Comments by employees about Randy Fields, Debbie Fields's husband, illustrate the philosophy of top management:

> "We are all driven by Randy's philosophy that he wants the organization to be as flat as possible," says Paul Quinn, the company's director of management information systems.
>
> "There are a few things," says controller Lynn Quilter, "that Randy dislikes about growth....He hates the thought of drowning in people so that he can't walk in and know exactly what each person does...The second thing that drives him nuts is paper."
>
> "The objective," says Randy, "is to leverage people—to get them to act when we have 1,000 stores the same way they acted when we had 30."
>
> "...if a machine can do it, a machine *should* do it. "People," says

Randy, "should do only that which people can do. It's demeaning for people to do what machines can do.

"...The other rule, the one that keeps the technological monster itself in check, is that the company will have but one data base. Don't enforce this rule, and, says Randy, "the next thing you know you have 48 different programs that can't talk to each other." (*Inc.*, October 1987, pp. 65-72.)

Technology has allowed Mrs. Fields to reduce boundaries between stores and headquarters; the technology has created an organization structure that feels flat despite having many layers of management. Electronic linking and communications make it easy to communicate across time zones using voice mail and e-mail. The technology affects the nature of work through detailed store operational control, freeing personnel for more sales work. Mrs. Fields can be more responsive to customers; it can change products and product mix through the systems running at headquarters and in the stores.

It is interesting to note that Mrs. Fields used IT to create a new organization. Her husband and business partner, Randy, was an IBM systems engineer at one point in his career. At Mrs. Fields, the opportunity to design a new organization combined with a senior manager with extensive experience with technology led to a nontraditional structure for part of the organization.

There have been management problems at Mrs. Fields. The firm expanded rapidly, possibly encouraged by the success of its technology, and ran into difficulty integrating its acquisition, La Petite Boulangerie, with its traditional cookie stores. While Mrs. Fields can change its mix of cookies easily, the original cookie operation is basically a one-product business. The firm is also reported to have had difficulties with its product and market mix when it entered international markets.

As the company expanded and tried to integrate La Petite Boulangerie, things did not go well.

But reality has a way of overmatching mythology, and the Fields cookie empire crumbled around the edges last year. The PCs that brought revolutionary management techniques to cookie stores weren't able to overcome the basic business realities of a limited, fickle market. Though Mrs. Fields officials dismiss the notion that fresh-baked cookies are a food fad gone stale, in 1988 the company lost money for the first time, and its stock, traded on the London Exchange, fell precipitously.

Now the Fieldses have placed PCs at the heart of a risky diversification into a new and potentially more stable business—full-service com-

mercial bakeries. They are "betting the company" that the business benefit of their cookie-store PC systems can reach beyond chocolate chips and
save the corporation....

"...The only reason we got into the bakery business was because we
thought our computer systems could get control of it," said Chairman
Randy Fields.

Over the next three years, Mrs. Fields will spend $50 million on La
Petite Boulangerie, a money-losing bakery-and-cafe chain it acquired in
1987. It will close nearly 100 of its 700 cookie stores and convert many
of them into combination cookie and bakery shops....

...But can a cookie-store technology cut it in the bakery-cafe world,
where inventories and consumer tastes are more complex? More important, can a cookie-cutter culture where PCs are boss pan out in a new
company that wasn't baked that way from scratch?

Fields and Quinn (director of IS) say yes on both counts. They said
the company's initial success in transferring its basic systems to "la Petite"
were, in fact, a main factor in the decision to invest $50 million more to
expand the bakery chain. Fields claims the systems "got control" of the
bakery chain enough to make it profitable 14 months after its acquisition." (*PC Week,* February 20, 1989)

In 1992, Randy Fields spun off a company called the Park City Group,
which specializes in selling the software made famous at Mrs. Fields. He
stepped down as CEO of Mrs. Fields Cookies to concentrate on the software
business, and eventually bought it from Mrs. Fields for $3.5 million. The sys-
tem has been adapted by Burger King and Skipper's Seafood chains. Phar-Mor
uses Field's payroll reporting system and has agreed to install the cash, sales, and
inventory reporting system that provides daily sales reports to management.

The March 1, 1993, issue of *Business Week* reported that Mrs. Fields "is
throwing in her apron. On February 17, Debbie Fields, who started her cook-
ie-making empire in Palo Alto, Calif., back in 1977, stepped down as president
and chief executive officer. Fields, who retains her position as chairwoman,
turned over nearly 80 percent of the company to four lenders led by Prudential
Insurance Co."

Is IT to blame at Mrs. Fields? Did the use of nontraditional organization
design strategies lead to Mrs. Fields giving up control of the business? It appears
that Mrs. Fields as an organization became overconfident of its abilities to manage businesses that were not a part of their core. A bakery chain like La Petite

Boulangerie is different from a cookie store. Did the technology lead management into a false sense of confidence and invulnerability?

Mrs. Fields illustrates a number of important points. The company used technology to coordinate headquarters and retail stores. Technology in the form of daily reporting systems made it possible for the store controller structure to be flat. The example shows that you can use technology to personalize and control the business: All Mrs. Fields stores look alike.

Mrs. Fields was very concerned about control and about quality; the technology helped her manage these two aspects of the business. Store controllers are a financial control mechanism. The combination of in-store computers, uniform recipes and cooking instructions, and uniform ingredients help provide quality control. Voice mail and e-mail helped motivate, and to some extent, control employees.

The technology allowed Debbie and Randy Fields to create different types of organization structures within the same firm. They could also "micromanage" what was happening at individual stores through the controllers at headquarters. The unanswered question is whether the technology helped lead top management away from their core business into ventures they did not understand well. Certainly this example illustrates that you have to manage all aspects of strategy and operations well; designing the world's best organization structure will not save the firm if its strategy or execution is fundamentally flawed.

VeriFone: The Virtual Corporation

William Melton founded VeriFone in 1981 to provide a simple check verification system; the company's products soon expanded to include credit card verification. In 1986 Hatim Tyabji joined VeriFone from Sperry to take command of a poorly performing company. Tyabji believed in a flexible organization structure and in the importance of being close to customers to provide a fast response to their needs (Galal 1995). The early history of VeriFone is described as "five people in four locations with almost no capital who grew a $400 million business world-wide" (presentation by Will Pape, former CIO and current advisor to the board, December, 1996). VeriFone faced strong competition in its early days from AT&T, GTE, Northern Telecom, and Mitsubishi, to name a few. In 1997 Hewlett-Packard acquired VeriFone in order to advance its efforts in electronic commerce; HP plans to keep VeriFone as an independent subsidiary.

VeriFone's mission is "to create and lead the transaction automation industry worldwide." In 1996 the company's products processed an estimated 65 percent to 70 percent of credit card transactions in the world. Much of the business is in custom software that runs in the verification "boxes" and on other parts of the transactions network. VeriFone offers over 1,600 programs that run on its verification devices. The firm has also formed alliances to verify and process payments on the Internet, including agreements with Netscape, several banks, and Discover. Since 1986 the company has had 36 continuously profitable quarters, with 25 percent sales growth per year on the average.

VeriFone does have an ongoing structure, similar to most organizations. What makes VeriFone unique, however, is the constant "organizing" that occurs within this structure that is accomplished through cross-functional teams. Any employee can form a task force to address a problem. The team makes a presentation to senior management; blue-collar workers have presented solutions to the CEO.

These teams come into and go out of existence regularly. They are virtual in the sense that they span different organizations and members may be in different locations. The constant formation, activity, and deactivation of teams is the mechanism through which VeriFone is constantly organizing. The formal organization structure is static while virtual teams create a dynamic, constantly changing organization.

In addition to teams within the firm, VeriFone forms alliances with other organizations. A virtual team might span organizational boundaries. In its early days, VeriFone tried to handle only core activities itself and outsource all others. Today the company has a number of alliances, including one with Microsoft to deliver commerce-enabled Internet products for retailers, and another with Digital Xpress to offer bundled ISDN services to various customers.

While organizing is a key activity at VeriFone, there is a conventional organization chart that shows reporting relationships and titles. The organization is relatively flat with the chairman having eight direct reports, the executive vice president, six. Tyabji's corporate model is a decentralized network of locations; he refers to this structure as the "blueberry pancake." "All berries are the same size; all locations are created equal" (Galal 1995). His least favorite location is corporate headquarters. (VeriFone tried to leave the "headquarters" blank empty on SEC filings, then tried "virtual," and finally had to enter "Redwood City.")

Regardless of formal structure, an employee can access any other employee directly through e-mail. The firm emphasizes the use of "point-to-point" communication using e-mail; one does not have to follow a hierarchy in order to communicate.

The focus is not on hierarchy and status. Rather, VeriFone defines the "right organization structure" as one locating employees near customers so that they continually put the customer first. The idea is that a customer in a country using VeriFone products can meet with a design engineer located in the customer's country; that design engineer can make changes in the product without approval from anyplace else. In 1997 VeriFone had 53 locations with 2,900 employees.

The chairman of VeriFone has very little use for politics. Senior management, however, does recognize that there are always questions about the degree of decentralization. What responsibilities should be vested in local units and what decisions should be centralized? Will Pape describes it as a "dynamic tension" to maintain control of the company, but to avoid having headquarters who dictate to local managers (personal communication, December 1996).

The management culture and norms at VeriFone allow it to operate in an organizing mode. Two of the key characteristics of VeriFone that emerged from discussions with company officials are "fast response" and "a culture of urgency." As one employee described it, there is "never time to rejoice" after finishing a project because there is always something else to do. A lack of organizational hierarchy makes it easier to respond quickly. The vice president of human resources felt quite comfortable giving a new employee the responsibility for coming up with a global profit-sharing plan in four months.

A manager who joined VeriFone from AT&T saw a new marketing program for smaller retailers develop over the VeriFone network in less than a week. By the end of the quarter the plan resulted in $2.7 million in new sales. It would have taken at least three months to come up with a similar program at any of the previous, traditionally organized companies where he had worked.

Because of geographic decentralization and the existence of many virtual teams, an employee is often on his or her own; it is not unusual to be located in Atlanta and to report to a supervisor in Paris. VeriFone counts on individual initiative to achieve its goals. An Internet engineer may come up with an idea unrelated to his current assignment. He should suggest this idea to others, and he may or may not be charged with following up on his initiative. VeriFone believes, according to its stated corporate philosophy, that those who perform a job know best how it should be done. It strives to involve employees in the management of their own areas of work. There is a three-year rolling strategic plan while a calendar year plan drives work assignments.

It is clear that this culture involves mutual trust. Employees trust the company to support their actions and to encourage experimentation. VeriFone trusts its employees to take initiative and act in the best interest of the company. VeriFone tries to maintain this culture with a minimum of rules.

Communications is a key activity at VeriFone. A corporate philosophy of distributing power to the lowest level of the organization possible reduces the amount of communications required to operate. At the same time, the global nature of VeriFone's operations creates significant demands for communications, especially for virtual project teams. Managers communicate with e-mail; there are no secretaries to print messages or enter responses. Executives in different countries might work together on the same spreadsheet in preparing a proposal. These executives can access information on bookings, shippings, and revenues from an on-line database with worldwide availability.

Pape believes that no single communications tool is always right for a particular job. VeriFone uses 32 different tools for communications. Travel, face-to-face meetings, and task forces are all communications mechanisms. Frequently task forces work "around the world" with conference calls scheduled so that members take turns at getting up at 2:00 A.M. to participate. To avoid overload, an effort is made to keep messages short and not bombard recipients with e-mail.

VeriFone stresses the need for employees, while a part of a virtual firm, to interact physically on a regular basis. Large rooms in local offices facilitate group gatherings, and the firm has annual meetings of different employees who work in similar functions. Every six to eight weeks, the senior management team gets together for a meeting in a different part of the world. (The vice president of human resources lives in Dallas; the former CIO and current advisor to the board has homes in Hawaii and Santa Fe, and the chairman lives in the San Francisco Bay Area.) Senior managers feel it is important for employees to know each other so they can use information technology effectively.

The cost of face-to-face communications is constant travel; Tyabji reports traveling over 400,000 miles in a year. About one-third of the company's employees are on the road at any one time, leading to an annual expenditure of over $5 million on hotels and airfare (Galal 1995).

VeriFone suggests that the virtual organization does not necessarily want to substitute electronic for physical interaction completely; rather the electronic and face-to-face communications complement each other. At VeriFone, occasional face-to-face communications enables more regular and routine electronic communications with its advantage of reducing the constraints of time and space on interaction.

In addition to communications mechanisms, VeriFone believes in sharing information. Will Pape prepares a daily "flash" report that goes to 300 VeriFone employees daily. The report is a method for evaluating progress. Recipients can easily access the data behind the interpretation so they are not dependent on one person's view of performance. Pape sees the role of the CIO as providing information and interpretation, not just data. He is the "navigator" who keeps senior management informed on a daily basis of whether the firm is on course.

Plans are posted throughout the company (including restroom stalls), and employees are encouraged to add comments to them. The company sends a video each quarter to employees' homes that includes amateur footage from various offices and countries. The firm provides so much information that it has registered more than 10 percent of its employees as "insiders" with the Federal Trade Commission. Employees' children are encouraged to communicate with their counterparts in other countries via e-mail.

VeriFone also shares information and knowledge with its customers and alliance partners. Before e-mail became easily available through service providers, VeriFone had suppliers and alliance partners on its own e-mail system. Today VeriFone provides videoconferencing equipment for these firms. Before going public when it had to be concerned about releasing information, VeriFone shared its daily "flash" report with some partners.

VeriFone uses "appropriate technology," not the newest equipment. It spends about 60 percent as much as comparable electronics firms on information technology. Its e-mail system runs on VAX computers and many users have not moved to graphical interfaces. The daily "flash" report is character-based. (One observer expressed concern that this low IT budget and modest infrastructure could prove to be a problem as the company expands in the future, especially if its business on the Internet becomes more important.) Current technology efforts include the development of an Intranet to facilitate information sharing. The responsibility for providing content on the Intranet will be distributed; for example, a new product group will create and maintain pages for its product.

For a VeriFone employee, the organizing character of the company, management culture and norms, and information sharing leads to self-governance. The employee may not have extensive physical contact with a supervisor. This employee is encouraged to take the initiative in coming up with new ideas for improving VeriFone, its products, and/or its service to customers. She will communicate using a variety of media with customers, alliance partners, and other

VeriFone employees. She may start a virtual, cross-functional team and be a member of several others. Her major focus will be on responsiveness and fast response to conditions in her local environment.

However, information technology means that she is not constrained to local solutions; VeriFone is able to marshal its global resources to solve local problems. An actual example helps to illustrate this global search. A customer told a sales representative in Greece, based on a VeriFone competitor's statements, that VeriFone lacked a certain product. The sales rep sent a single e-mail to "ISales," which reached all sales reps worldwide, asking whether VeriFone had a product for this customer. A sales manager in San Francisco took on the task of heading this virtual task force. He collated 100 replies and constructed a Powerpoint presentation for the sales rep in Greece (while the rep slept). The sales manager had the presentation translated to Greek, and the sales rep took it to his client the next day. VeriFone won the account.

A combination of management structure, culture, and technology provide the opportunity for a virtual organization like VeriFone to manage through self-governance. At the same time, the technology makes it possible to bring the global resources of the firm to bear on local (or global) problems wherever they arise.

Calyx and Corolla: Building a New Firm with IT

An entrepreneur named Ruth Owades founded Calyx and Corolla. Before starting C&C, she was successful introducing a new distribution channel for gardening products. Owades founded a company called Gardener's Eden, a mail-order business for gardening tools and accessories. After a few years, she sold the business to Williams-Sonoma and operated Gardener's Eden for over four years as a division of Sonoma.

Four years later, Owades decided to launch Calyx and Corolla after careful research. Her first observation was about how inefficient the flower and plant market was in the United States. Flower and plant sales in the United States run to $10 billion annually, with a substantial proportion of the flowers imported from countries like Colombia and the Netherlands.

The distribution channel to retail florists is lengthy and involves a number of parties. Typically a grower sends flowers to distributors in a growing region. From there, the flowers go to various wholesalers who distribute the product to florists, supermarkets, and other retailers.

Owades's insight was that she could dramatically "reengineer" this distribution process if she could negotiate agreements with growers and a carrier to deliver flowers directly to the consumer. She wanted to eliminate all of the steps and organizations between the grower and the consumer. While this idea was appealing, there were many in the industry who thought it impossible.

Owades, a master saleswoman, worked with growers encouraging them to experiment with her. One acquaintance, Peter Barr at Sunbay Growers, entered a test with Owades. They tried shipping flowers via retail carriers in different kinds of packages. The experiment showed that it was feasible to package flowers for this kind of shipment.

Owades knew that she needed two things to be credible with parties who might provide financing. The first was a group of growers willing to make arrangements and package flowers for delivery to the end customer, a new role for the grower. A number of growers responded positively to her approach because they were looking for additional distribution channels and were sensitive to growing foreign competition. Second, Owades knew that she needed a first-class overnight delivery firm to lend credibility to her new business. She campaigned to interest management at Federal Express in the concept. At that time, FedEx was campaigning for more mail-order delivery business, and eventually they agreed to deliver flowers for Calyx and Corolla. Owades had to guarantee that she would cover damage from packages left without a signature to finalize the deal.

Owades and her management team decided that the best way to interest the consumer was with an upscale catalog that contained appealing photos of arrangements and plants along with information about the plants. The catalog had to be interesting reading. By 1991, Calyx and Corolla was mailing over 12 million catalogs annually.

The final component to make Calyx and Corolla work was information technology. The entire concept depends on electronic linking and communications between customers, Calyx and Corolla, growers, and Federal Express. A staff in a San Francisco suburb answers calls on an 800 number and charges merchandise to the caller's credit card. Several times a day, C&C transmits orders via modem or FAX to growers. Each grower appointed a Calyx and Corolla account manager to supervise order printing, the selection and packing of flowers, the writing of gift messages, and the preparation of FedEx shipping papers.

Federal Express picks up the orders at the end of the day and delivers the flowers the next morning anyplace in the Continental United States. Calyx and Corolla must maintain a computer system to process orders and to select orders for transmission to growers based on the customer's desired delivery date. C&C must also handle accounting; it has to remit to the growers and to Federal

Express. Finally, it submits its credit card receipts to the appropriate card processing company.

We have called Calyx and Corolla an example of a "negotiated agreement" organization. Calyx and Corolla itself is relatively small. It has a number of virtual components, including a production and inventory facility (the grower), a highly computerized logistics and delivery system (Federal Express), an accounts receivables operation (credit card companies), and a large sales force (the catalog). Ruth Owades started Calyx and Corolla by "snapping together" various virtual components coordinated by information technology.

Oticon: A Radical, Team-Based Structure

Oticon has positioned itself to be the preferred partner for leading hearing-aid clinics around the world. It has recently developed a breakthrough digital hearing aid that contains the world's smallest microprocessor, according to the firm. This award-winning hearing aid amplifies just the frequencies at which the user has difficulty hearing, and amplifies them only as much as necessary.

Oticon headquarters are in the Tuborg Industrial Park in northern Copenhagen. There are three manufacturing facilities in Denmark and other countries. The company began producing its own hearing aids during World War II. It was family owned until 1956, when new management took over and began mass production of hearing aids. By the end of the 1970s Oticon had reached the number-one position in the world market with a 15 percent share and sales in over 100 countries. It was a leader in miniaturization for hearing aids worn behind the ear.

However, from 1979 through 1985, Oticon's market share dropped from 15 percent to 7 percent as competitors developed hearing aids that fit inside the ear. The company had losses in 1986 and 1987, and the board recruited a new president, Lars Kolind, in 1988. His first action was to start a cost-cutting program in an attempt to regain profitability. Kolind also changed the firm's marketing strategy. For years, Oticon had stressed high-quality hearing aids, but now competitors were also building quality units. Kolind decided that the most appropriate strategy for Oticon was quality *and* customer satisfaction. Oticon would focus its business on dispensers or retailers of hearing aids who were most interested in producing satisfied customers.

After two years, Kolind realized that cost-cutting and a new marketing strategy had accomplished about all they could.

> I sat down on New Year's Day…and tried to think the unthinkable; a
> vision for the company of tomorrow. It would be a company where jobs

were shaped to fit the person instead of the other way around. Each person would be given more functions and a job would emerge by the individual accumulating a portfolio of functions (Bjorn-Andersen and Turner, 1994).

Kolind wanted to transform Oticon from an industrial organization producing a standardized product to a "high quality service organization with a physical product." He envisioned an organization in which various functional units worked together in an integrated manner to develop innovative products. Kolind realized that he would have to create a new, flexible organization.

Kolind wrote a memo describing Oticon as one team of 150 employees at headquarters, all continuously developing and learning new skills. Each employee should be able to do several tasks: those he or she already did well and those where the employee would be challenged to learn new tasks. The idea was not to focus on functional expertise, but for each person to be able to do several jobs. Kolind also felt that paper hindered efficiency; paper hides information instead of sharing it. He imagined computer systems that would eliminate paper and allow all employees to share information.

Kolind called his new plan a "spaghetti organization" because he envisioned people playing multiple, intertwined roles in the firm. To begin with, he combined two separate offices into a new building designed for his new organization. Unlike many business process redesign projects, Kolind invited the participation of his employees in designing the new organization. It should be noted that, at first, there was a great deal of resistance to Kolind's proposals. When Kolind backed off from a plan to move headquarters to Jutland, a remote part of Denmark, and chose instead to locate in the Tuborg Industrial Park, resistance faded. It is clear that the changes at Oticon would not have happened without Kolind's strong and forceful leadership.

The first step was to eliminate traditional departments. The head office became one large department, and work was organized as projects. Oticon views projects as temporary; employees with different skills work together on different projects. This team-oriented arrangement works very well when the workload is uneven. In a more rigid structure, the marketing department would have to be staffed to handle its heavy load in the fall for exhibitions and trade shows. In the new structure, the marketing task becomes a project and enough resources are acquired to complete it. Normally about five people work consistently on marketing tasks; when the busy season arrives, this core group recruits other employees with different backgrounds, like R&D, to help out.

The second major innovation was to organize work in the form of projects. There are a project manager and a number of other employees who work on the project. The project manager has responsibility for staffing the team and for carrying out the task. A project manager advertises the project on an electronic bulletin board on the Oticon system; employees at their workstations sign up for a project.

Employees occupy several positions at Oticon depending on the number and variety of projects for which they volunteer. This approach to organizing takes maximum advantage of diversity; an employee in accounting might sign up for a project involving marketing, bringing a whole new perspective to the marketing project.

To be successful, Oticon had to adopt a new philosophy of control. Management has to trust employees to sign up for projects; this voluntarism should result in greater commitment to the firm and to more worker responsibility. Managers spend less time monitoring workers; instead managers must be innovators and motivators.

To bring about this new structure, Oticon had to rearrange its physical and technology domains. First, Kolind eliminated all private offices, including his own. All employees have identical desks and chairs in a large open space. There is a workstation and a mobile phone charger on the desks. Desks are not assigned; a worker moves his or her small, lockable caddie to a desk. The caddie has a drawer for personal items and shelves for storing up to 10 files. Access to information is gained through the workstation.

Kolind also wanted to banish paper; Oticon's technology eliminates 95 percent of the paper in the office. The company scans all documents as they are received, and workers are prohibited from keeping paper files. Original documents are shredded. All of this information is stored in electronic form, and users can retrieve it from their workstations, given that they have access rights.

When an employee enters his or her ID into the workstation, the system is configured with that individual's electronic desktop. The system has tools for creating, transmitting, and storing documents containing text, drawings, and graphics. This combination of physical and electronic flexibility makes it possible to create task forces almost immediately to solve a problem.

Oticon has enjoyed a return to profitability; 1992 profits were nine times better than those of 1989 and 1990. Sales are increasing, and the company has reduced its cycle time to market new products. A new hearing aid that adjusts itself to the level of ambient sound was brought to market six months earlier than it could have been without the new organization.

Oticon demonstrates technological leveling, using the technology to reduce layers of management and substitute work groups. This approach also changes the role of the manager, making this person much more of a leader than a person who monitors employees. Information technology helps form the project teams, facilitates communications, and provides tools to team members to help accomplish their tasks. Oticon has created a highly flexible and virtual organization through process redesign combined with information technology.

Summary and Implications

This chapter has presented five different organizations that have invested in technology to change their structure and operations. Figure 8-1 portrays the structure of each of these firms after implementing new IT. Management chose the various structures in all cases but Frito-Lay, and designed technology to facilitate them. In the case of Frito-Lay, managers realized that technology designed for one purpose could be used for other aspects of managing the company. Gradually, the structure of the firm changed to take advantage of this new technological capability.

Figure 8–2
IT-Enabled Organization Forms

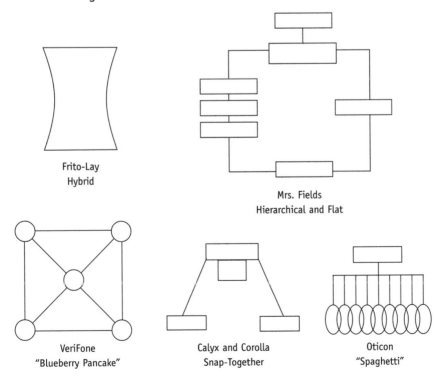

Frito-Lay
Hybrid

Mrs. Fields
Hierarchical and Flat

VeriFone
"Blueberry Pancake"

Calyx and Corolla
Snap-Together

Oticon
"Spaghetti"

Mrs. Fields used technology to create a flat financial control structure while maintaining a traditional, hierarchical sales organization. At VeriFone, the technology investment is less than for comparable electronics firms, and it is targeted at communications and information sharing, which are crucial to a global, virtual firm. IT allowed Calyx and Corolla to coordinate alliance partners, virtual components that made it possible to start the firm quickly. C&C did not have to build a production facility, distribution network, or accounts receivable; it could form partnerships and link with these components using technology.

Table 8-1

Summary of Transformational IT Investments

Investment	Results	Observations
Frito-Lay	Began with $40 million for hand-held computers; evolved to change operations and management	Frito-Lay created a hybrid organization with old and new features; it has decentralized decision-making to lower levels of the firm through technology
Mrs. Fields Cookies	Technology used for all aspects of control, both financial and product quality	A dual structure that is hierarchical for sales and flat for financial control
VeriFone	"Appropriate" technology facilitates communications and information-sharing	VeriFone is a true virtual organization
Calyx and Corolla	Technology coordinates different virtual components	C&C built a new organization by snapping together different components, several of which are virtual
Oticon	The company developed technology to facilitate flexible work assignments and a team-based organization	Technology is the glue that holds Oticon's teams together; it makes it possible to coordinate work and track progress

Oticon developed IT that would let it form flexible project teams and reconfigure its headquarters whenever new opportunities arose (see Table 8-1).

The companies do not publish figures about their investments in information technology. Except for Mrs. Fields, each of these firms has been very successful financially. Determining what part of their success is due to their investments in IT to calculate an ROI seems an impossible assignment. While we were able to value investments in IT with a direct return in Chapter 4, the kinds of IT investments made by the firms in this chapter *are a component of a much larger management effort to change the organization.* Taken alone, the IT investment might make a difference as it did at Frito-Lay. However, without Lars Kolind's vision for a new Oticon, the company would probably never have invested in IT to support a team-based organization. The success of these companies comes from management, employees, products and services, and many other factors, including investments in information technology.

If it is so difficult to determine a return on these investments, how do managers decide to make them? We will discuss this question more fully in Chapter 10. However, it is quite likely that the managers involved in the companies in this chapter saw technology as the solution to a problem. Calyx and Corolla needed a production facility and distribution system; communicating with growers electronically was necessary because it provided the fastest response to customers. VeriFone developed technology as it was needed to coordinate far-flung operations and to communicate with customers. Managers wanted to change existing or create new organizations; investing in IT was a mechanism for accomplishing their goals.

PART IV

Increasing the Chances for Successful Investment

Conversion effectiveness is an important filter in the garbage can model; it determines whether an IT investment will be successfully implemented. If the firm fails to develop an application, as many have, there is little or no chance of obtaining a return on its investment. Chapter 9 discusses some of the risks and alternative approaches available to management for implementing IT.

Chapter 10 is extremely important: It draws on all of the evidence and arguments to date to suggest how management can make good IT investment decisions. While discussing two economic evaluation models, the chapter stresses the overall context of making IT investment decisions. It suggests that a variety of information is needed in order to make wise decisions; it is particularly important for management to have a strategy and a vision for technology in the firm. Because there is such variety in the sources of value from IT, the decision maker needs considerable information. The chapter suggests what information is most important and presents a format for displaying it. Those making decisions should look at past, current, and proposed IT investment decisions in allocating resources to technology

CHAPTER NINE

Perspectives on Conversion Effectiveness

I*n the garbage can model,* conversion effectiveness is a major filter for IT investments; it determines whether the organization can expect to implement its technology initiatives successfully. We have seen one study that found empirical support for the importance of conversion effectiveness. If the organization fails to implement an IT initiative, there will be no value. If the implementation is only partially effective, then the return from the investment will be less than originally anticipated.

Figure 9-1 presents one view of conversion effectiveness. Within the organization, the cast of characters is generally broken into three groups: managers, users, and the IT staff. Managers are responsible for deciding on an IT investment, and users (and many managers) will come in contact with the applications resulting from the investment. The problem addressed by the investment is extremely important in influencing conversion effectiveness. How important is the problem? How widespread? The nature of the problem and the firm's resources will influence its strategy for developing an application. This strategy involves the selection of the type of IT labor applied to the problem. The results of applying IT labor and capital, the execution of the initiative, results in a problem solution. This solution is expected to result in changes in the organization, and quite possibly in the relationship between the investing organization and other organizations. The IT infrastructure supports the development and ongoing operation of the IT initiative.

In the rest of this chapter, we explore the various parts of Figure 9-1 to develop strategies for increasing the chances for the conversion of an IT investment into a successful application.

Figure 9–1

A View of Conversion Effectiveness

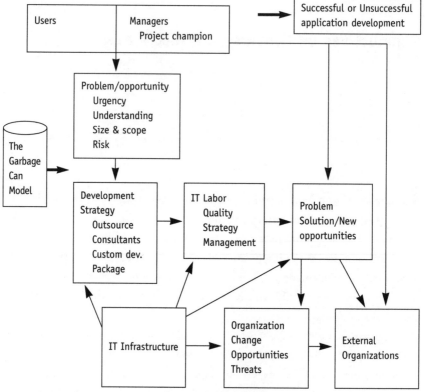

Users and Managers: The Force Behind the Investment

In the early days of technology, managers authorized new projects and users worked with the IT staff to develop them. A lucky manager would move on to a new assignment before the new application appeared. In today's environment, managers and users all interact with workstations and a variety of systems. The only real distinction may be that managers have responsibility for the investment and for conversion effectiveness.

Table 9-1 shows some of the activities involved in turning an IT investment into an application. Managers and users are critical in all phases of the conversion. Managers may generate the idea for an investment. Even if they do not, they need to create an environment that encourages others to take the initiative and suggest new ideas. The manager cannot be expected to develop every creative idea; his or her responsibility is to nurture creativity and to recognize a good idea when it comes along. VeriFone provides a good example of a com-

Table 9-1

Shared Responsibilities in Conversion

Activity	Managers	Users	IT Staff
Generating the idea for an investment	Come up with ideas; create environment for others to make suggestions	Look for opportunities	Present success stories from other firms; look for models in other industries
Evaluating the investment	Identify benefits	Identify benefits	Estimate costs
Choosing an implementation option	Outline options	Evaluate options	Evaluate options
Developing problem solution	Be a project champion; monitor and manage project	Participate in project; understand solution	Understand problem and solution; participate in developing solution
Changing the organization	Lead change effort	Participate in change	Participate in change
Determining relationship with other organizations	Establish linkages with external organizations	Coordinate with external organizations	Connect to external organizations
Evaluation	Establish criteria	Evaluate results	Evaluate results

pany that expects and rewards initiative; innovation is a part of everyone's job. The IT staff here can contribute by publicizing examples of successful IT investments, particularly in your industry. Sometimes an idea from another industry applies to yours as well. For example, Allegiance's order entry applications are generic, as are many Web applications for customer service.

Chapter 10 is devoted to the topic of evaluating potential investments in IT; at this point we can say that all parties will be involved in this activity. Much of the book has established the foundation for the recommendations in Chapter 10 on what kind of evaluation is appropriate for each type of IT investment in the Investment Opportunities Matrix of Chapter 1.

There are a number of ways to implement an investment in IT. The ultimate responsibility for the choice belongs to management. Managers, however, will need help in delineating and evaluating alternatives. The important thing is that today one has a number of choices; traditional development with a team of systems analysts and programmers is only one option.

One of the keys to success with an IT project is developing the problem solution. There is some evidence to suggest that the most important role for management in this stage is to be a champion of a project. In the case of Frito-Lay, the hand-held computer project was placed on hold when the main sponsor moved to another job in Pepsico, Frito-Lay's owner. When this manager returned to Frito-Lay, he started the project again. The investment was extremely successful; it is surprising that no one else in the organization saw enough potential to assume sponsorship when this manager left. The manager has to be the champion; there is no one else in a position to assume this role.

In addition to being the sponsor, managers have to monitor and manage projects. It is easy, as we have seen, for projects to spin out of control; some are canceled and others experience cost and time overruns. The user has to participate in developing a solution to the problem addressed, and so does the IT staff, depending on the option chosen for implementation.

Organization change falls clearly to management and users. In Chapters 8, the four companies that planned change and then chose technology to support it did a good job of managing change. Sometimes the problem solution will involve other organizations like customers and suppliers; managers have to establish the necessary links while users and the IT staff make the connection.

After implementation, the organization will learn more from the development effort if it evaluates the results. Estimating the actual return on investment, organization change, and/or indirect benefits that might result from an application provides the organization with an idea of the value of its IT investment.

The Nature of the Problem or Opportunity

The problem or opportunity addressed by an investment in IT has a tremendous impact on conversion effectiveness. The initiative may have considerable urgency, such as a competitive application. When UPS learned that FedEx was going to allow package tracking on its Web site, the comparable project at UPS undoubtedly received a high priority.

This example also illustrates issues of size and scope. The package-tracking application no doubt is challenging. One has to connect a Web interface with a legacy mainframe database. However, this activity is so popular now that there are many products from different vendors that facilitate such linkages. The scope of the project was narrow and relatively well defined. On the other hand, consider the implementation of a large enterprise-wide application like SAP's R/3 throughout a company the size of Lucent Technologies. The chairman of Lucent has stated that he expects the organization to save $1 billion a year in operating expenses from this application. (Unfortunately, Lucent has not published their investment figures.) The size and scope of this application is enormous; Lucent has well in excess of 100,000 employees at various locations.

All of the characteristics of the problem or investment opportunity contribute to project risk. There are few studies of risk, but it seems logical that large projects with unknown technology have the highest uncertainty associated with them. Some of the development strategies discussed in the next section are intended to reduce these risks, though they can never be completely eliminated.

One of the best ways to reduce project risk is for everyone involved to develop a thorough understanding of the problem addressed by the IT investment. Technology is very abstract; it is hard for individuals to see and understand what an application will do. Companies often build small prototypes of a system to help potential users visualize how an application will work. Other techniques include frequent group meetings in which a group of designers present the logic of an application to users and managers. *Managers, users, and IT staff members need to realize that developing an understanding of what an IT application is intended to accomplish is critical for success.*

Development Strategies

The strategy one chooses for development has a direct impact on the level of investment required for an IT initiative (see Table 9-2). In the early years of information technology, most applications employed custom development. A manager authorized a new system, and the IT staff took over; this group interviewed users, wrote specifications, and created programs to match the specifications. The advantage of this development model is the ability it provides to include all of the functions desired in the system; the organization develops a system that is customized for its needs. The disadvantage is the length of time and the cost of custom development. Often, in order to meet budget and time constraints, developers had to sacrifice features of the system, and then users did not have all of the functions they requested. As custom development projects grew in complexity, the uncertainty of successful completion also grew.

One strategy is to hire external expertise, either to develop the entire application or to work with the internal IT staff. Consultants have been available for

Table 9-2

Development Strategies

Alternative	Pros	Cons
Custom development	Include all functions and features would like to have; internal staff knows existing systems; firm maintains control	Very time-consuming and costly; many examples of project failure and projects that do not meet specifications
Consultants	Provide additional help; may assume entire responsibility or contribute some component of application; often have expertise lacking in the organization	Costly; there can be difficult relations between company employees and outside consultants; consulting firms also have examples of failed projects
Outsourcing	Firm gets a contractual agreement with an outsourcer who should have great expertise with technology	Outsourcing agreement can be hard to negotiate and/or monitor; managers still have to be involved in managing the outsourcing agreement
Packages	Today, often the first choice is to buy rather than to build; user obtains debugged code that has been used elsewhere; today's packages are considerably better than original efforts; in general, package implementation will be faster than custom development	Packages may lack some of the functions you need; they can be very difficult and expensive to implement (e.g., SAP); you may have to change your organization to use the package if changing the package is not an option

developing IT investments since the first systems appeared. Consultants will provide advice, and many will actually undertake the development of the IT application. Carried to an extreme, the firm can outsource the development and even the operation of an IT application. For example, Calyx and Corolla outsourced its delivery and logistics to FedEx; C&C took advantage of the package-tracking technology that FedEx had already developed. There are a number of network providers who offer complete EDI services, and a firm might outsource its electronic data interchange efforts to them.

The major advantage of consultants and outsourcing is the external expertise available. SAP is so complex and difficult to implement that most firms include a budget for help from a consulting firm that has extensive experience with this package. When the firm enters into a consulting or outsourcing agreement for a technology initiative, it should be aware of the need to *manage* its relationship with the outsourcer. Firms that have delegated the responsibility for developing a new IT application to an outside firm generally have been unhappy with the results. Managers still have to monitor the agreement and work with the outsourcer. There are examples of many very elaborate management committees and structures established at firms like Kodak and Xerox to manage outsourced IT.

Today, most organizations seek to find a package they can buy before turning to custom development. If the package is available, one can usually visit firms that have implemented it to see the system work. One does not have to be content with abstract design specifications; you can see a working system. The package code is already running, so it should have far fewer errors than custom code developed for a project. Since the software exists, implementing a packaged solution should also be faster than custom development.

There are several drawbacks to packages. First, the package may not have exactly the features you need, and many vendors do not want to customize their software for each buyer. (Such customization creates maintenance problems for the package vendor as it develops new releases and updates for the package.) Implementing a major package is not simple; there may be hundreds or thousands of decisions and values to be entered into tables before the package will run. For large packages, you may be expected to change your method of doing business to fit the package rather than modify the package. On balance, the package route seems to have more factors in favor than other development strategies.

IT Labor

The quality of the IT staff is an important factor in conversion effectiveness. The labor market for professionals in this field is very tight, making it hard to attract and retain competent staff. In addition to staff quality, management has to have a strategy for organizing IT labor and for managing individual projects. Strategies for IT labor include consideration of such issues as the structure of development teams, the technologies to be used in developing an application, the nature and extent of non-IT staff members on a project team, to name a few. IT management also needs a strategy for motivating and developing the IT staff. It is responsible for establishing an approach to formal project management.

There are different views of how this team should function and manage a project. Software engineering provides a methodical approach to developing specifications and programming. It stresses the need for specifications that users and managers can easily understand. Software engineering also includes conventions for writing computer programs so that the code is well structured, which makes it easier to debug and change.

The latest approach to improving productivity is object-oriented technologies. Object orientation can be applied in both design of a system and in programming. The logical focus of this approach is an object, for example, an invoice. Various methods that operate on that object are encapsulated with it; these methods are pieces of program code. The idea is to think at a high level of abstraction about objects, and to keep program code with the object it affects to prevent unintended changes.

There has been too little experience with object-oriented approaches to know if they are demonstrably better than more traditional ways to develop systems. Comparing approaches is difficult. In an experiment the task is likely to be too small to generalize the results. It is difficult to find anyone who wants to develop a large project twice, using two different methodologies to compare the results!

The Role of an IT Infrastructure

The nature of a firm's IT infrastructure also has a major impact on conversion effectiveness in at least two ways. First, the infrastructure provides the resources available for a new initiative. Suppose that senior management has decided that the firm should offer customers the ability to review and order its products on the World Wide Web. The size and scope of this initiative will vary according to whether the company has a home page and other information on the Web, whether it has an Intranet, or whether it has experience at all with HTML and the WWW. Similarly, if the firm wants to develop a client-server application and has only mainframe computers, it will have a much more difficult time than a firm that has already invested in client-server technology.

The issue here is not just one of investment, it also involves learning and time. There is a learning curve, sometimes quite steep, with new technology. If the firm has not developed a modern infrastructure over time, it will have to invest more for a new IT initiative because of the need to build infrastructure. It will also have a longer development time as the IT staff learns about this infrastructure and develops the new applications that require it.

The second way infrastructure impacts the development of a new application is the possible need for more investment in infrastructure to develop a new IT initiative. The question of how to account for additional infrastructure expense is a difficult one. Investment clearly associated with a new initiative, for example, the need to add a new server to host a Web-based ordering application, should be a part of the investment for the project. However, if the firm has no Web presence and must learn how to use the Internet for the first time, should that cost be a part of the current initiative, or does it belong in some kind of shared infrastructure cost category?

Problem Solution or Opportunity

The reason for undertaking the investment is to take advantage of a new opportunity or to solve a problem. All of the factors discussed previously impact the success of the effort to convert the IT investment into an application. Problems with any of these aspects of conversion can lead to outright project failures or to projects that do not meet specifications, as described in Chapter 2. Under these conditions, the firm will get less for its investment in IT than originally planned.

Suppose that an IT initiative is expected to cost $100,000 and be finished in one year. The company expects to save $20,000 the first year and in each succeeding year and its cost of capital is 15 percent. Even without discounting, the project looks like a good investment. However, suppose that problems with implementing the initiative lead to savings of $10,000 a year instead of $20,000. Would you undertake the project now? Of course, if the project fails completely, there will be no benefits at all.

Organization Change

We undertake investments in IT to change the organization. The change may be very minor, such as the replacement of one system with a new one offering additional functions and a more pleasant user interface. The degree of change required here is relatively low. An investment like SAP requires major organizational changes in work processes and in the tasks individuals perform. The success of the investment not only depends on the factors described earlier, but on the change effort as well. Changing the organization may be as much of a challenge as developing the application.

Change is also an opportunity. For most of the companies discussed in Chapter 8, management decided on a desired organization structure and used IT investments to help create it. Managers planned for change and welcomed it as an opportunity to make the entire organization function better. Change is always a threat, as we are forced to alter behavior that has been successful until now. However, as we have seen in some of the examples in this book, change is also an opportunity to reshape the organization and make it more competitive.

The Role of External Organizations

The push toward greater connectivity is a major factor driving IT investments today. The federal government has mandated a certain level of EDI compliance for companies that wish to do business with it. Industry associations encourage companies to communicate electronically. Efficient customer response, EDI, JIT, continuous replenishment programs, and the Internet are all examples of different kinds of electronic connectivity.

Many IT investments will involve linking with other organizations, which means that a manager has to worry about coordinating a project with outside firms. External groups consist of customers and suppliers. A firm might decide to implement electronic commerce through a Web store set up by Open Market, an Internet service provider. It will have to manage its relationships with this vendor and with customers who eventually use the Internet to place orders.

I visited a distribution firm that was committed to EDI transactions for all of its purchases. This firm's IT staff spent much of its time helping suppliers develop their own EDI capabilities; its IT staff was consulting (for no fee) with its suppliers. This distributor felt the benefits of EDI were great enough that it was willing to invest in helping its suppliers develop the necessary capabilities. External organizations in this case were critical to the success of the distributor's EDI effort.

Summary

Conversion effectiveness refers to the process of turning an investment in IT into a working application. This chapter has discussed some of the factors that influence effectiveness. In the garbage can model, conversion effectiveness is the filter through which an investment in IT must pass before one obtains value from an IT initiative.

Most approaches to evaluating IT investments assume 100 percent conversion effectiveness. In Chapter 2 we introduced the idea that there are other probabilities for conversion success; in fact, the probability ranges from 0 to 1.0. It would be interesting to go back in time to the initial decision to invest in the Air Traffic Control Modernization Project or the IRS Modernization effort to see if, looking at the objectives of the project, one could come up with a reasonable estimate of the probability for successful conversion. Would our estimates have been close to the actual 0 percent?

The purpose of this chapter has been to demonstrate why one should question the assumption that conversion effectiveness is 100 percent when looking at a new investment opportunity. The chapter has described some of the many factors that contribute to successful conversion. Thinking about these components in advance can help estimate the probability of success, an important consideration in computing the expected value from an investment in IT.

CHAPTER TEN

Implications for the IT Investment Decision

At this point I hope this book has presented sufficient evidence to establish that:

1. there is value from investing in information technology;
2. each type of investment has a potentially different opportunity for a payoff, and for some applications, we may not be able to show a quantitative return;
3. the process of moving from the investment to an actual IT initiative is filtered by conversion effectiveness; there have been widely varying degrees of success in developing applications from IT investments.

If the estimate of 50 percent of U.S. capital investment being in technology is accurate, managers frequently face a decision on whether to invest and what amount to invest in IT. What does our discussion so far suggest about the investment decision?

The manager needs to keep the above-mentioned findings in mind. They suggest that in making decisions about IT investment, you should:

1. determine the type of investment, e.g., infrastructure or competitive necessity;
2. estimate the likely return from the investment given its type;
3. estimate the probability that there will be a return;
4. estimate the probability of successfully converting the investment into an application;
5. consider the possible upside benefits that might come from the investment;

6. compute the probability of a successful return (the S/R index) using the IT Investment Equation (Chapter 2) as another piece of information about the portfolio of IT investments in the organization;
7. look at the expected value from the investment by applying the IT Value Equation (Chapter 2).

This approach is both quantitative and qualitative. For some types of IT investments, you will have to rely more on qualitative arguments because potential benefits are hard to measure and to estimate. In other cases, there are well-known capital budgeting approaches one can apply to provide some guidance on the investment. For the reader who is not interested in capital budgeting, particularly net present value analysis or options pricing models, I recommend skipping the next few sections and going directly to the section of the chapter entitled "Guidelines for IT Investments."

Traditional Net Present Value Analysis

Probably the most frequently used capital budgeting analysis is based on net present value (NPV). The concept takes into account the time value of money and the likelihood that an investment will pay returns over some period of time. Assume that you are offered $1000 today or $1075 in one year. If the annual interest rate is 10 percent, which of these offers would you prefer? The first offer is best because you can take the $1000 and invest it at 10 percent, which will yield $1100 in one year's time. You are likely to be indifferent between $1000 now and $1100 a year from now.

Suppose now that the interest rate falls to 8 percent and you are asked how much money you would need to invest today to have $1400 in one year. How would you solve this problem? In the first example, you were given $1000 and an interest rate of 10 percent. To find the value of this investment in one year, you multiplied the $1000 by 1 plus the interest rate, or 1.10, giving $1100. To solve for the principal given the ending value, then, you divide that ending value by 1 plus the interest rate. A sum of $1400 divided by 1 plus 0.08 is $1400/1.08 = $1296. You have to invest $1296 today at 8 percent interest to have $1400 in one year.

What would happen if the investment is for two years? How much would you need to invest today at 8 percent to have $1400 in two years? To get to the beginning of the second year, you would divide by 1.08. Then, to get to the beginning of the first year, you would divide again by 1.08 giving a result of $1200. To check, at the end of the first year, $1200 invested at 8 percent has grown to $1296. Interest during the second year will be 8 percent on $1296, which gives $1400. As shown below, in the top line from left to right, one applies the interest rate to the principal to get the compounded balance at the end of year 2. In the second line, from right to left, one applies the discount factor to get the present value of $1400 in year 2 at the beginning of year 0.

Year 0		Year 1		Year 2
$1200	→ × 1.08 →	$1296	→ × 1.08 →	$1400
$1200	← × 1/1.08 ←	$1296	← × 1/1.08 ←	$1400

These examples lead to the formula for present value, or PV factor, for a sum n periods in the future at interest rate i:

$$PV = \frac{1}{(1 + i)^n}$$

To calculate the present value of a sum S, multiply it by the formula for present value. With present value, you are discounting future income to today taking into account the time value of money. If you have two investments that have different costs and different income streams, present value is a way to compare them.

Assume that two managers each suggest an IT investment. Project A requires an investment of $45,000 today, and will pay off $20,000 at the end of this year and $30,000 at the end of next year. Project B costs $30,000 today, and will pay $50,000 at the end of the third year. To compare these two projects, the first thing we need is a discount or interest rate. Assume that the company's cost of capital is 10 percent. For Project A, we need to discount the two payoffs, $20,000 and $30,000.

$20,000 at the end of year 1 has a PV of 20,000/1.10 = $18,182
$30,000 at the end of year 2 has a PV of 30,000/(1.10 × 1.10) = $24,793

The sum of the two present values is $42,975; this is the income stream from Project A discounted to today. For project B, we have income of $50,000 at the end of year 3:

$50,000 at the end of year 3 has a PV of 50,000/(1.10 × 1.10 × 1.10) = $37,566.

We see that Project A has a higher present value from its payoffs than Project B ($42,975 compared with $37,566). Does that mean the company should invest in Project A? These numbers represent the returns on the investment; they have to be compared with a project's cost. The net present value does this comparison. Project A costs $45,000 today; its net present value is $42,975 - $45,000, or -$2025. Project B has an NPV of $37,566 - $30,000, or $7566. The firm should therefore undertake Project B on the basis of estimated costs and benefits (disregarding other factors). In general, one should not make investments with a negative net present value, as you are not earning the return specified in the interest rate used in the calculation.

The formula for net present value, or, NPV is:

$$NPV = -C + \sum_{t=1}^{T} \frac{At}{(1+i)^t}$$

where C is the initial investment cost (possibly a stream of investments discounted to the present time period), A is the income at time period t, i is the interest rate, and T is the project life.

Net present value has a number of advantages when used in capital budgeting. You can discount both returns and costs to the present time to arrive at the net present value of a project. Since NPV is frequently used as a basis for evaluating a variety of corporate investments, decision makers will have comparable information to use in allocating capital. It is relatively straightforward to compute using a spreadsheet package.

There are some problems applying this technique to IT investments, however. It is difficult to estimate both the costs and the revenues or savings for an IT investment compared to investments like the purchase of a new machine for a factory. NPV analysis also assumes that predicted benefits will actually occur; it does not allow for problems with conversion effectiveness. In general, NPV assumes that the interest rate is constant and has no variability. Since some types of IT investments, like those for infrastructure, may have little payoff now, and a highly uncertain benefit in the future, NPV is biased against funding these kinds of initiatives.

Net present value does not explicitly consider risk. We have introduced this concept in computing expected values before applying NPV. However, considerations of risk are outside of the model. NPV has been accused of discriminating against longer-term and more risky programs because of this failure. Our estimates of expected value come to a single number; an investment analysis that actually looked at the distribution of possible benefits and costs would be more realistic. Finally, NPV does not deal with the implications of *not* undertaking an investment. For a system that is necessary to meet the competition, what are the benefits? Should we estimate the payoff as incremental revenue or the value of the market share lost if the firm fails to make an investment in technology?

Many analysts feel that IT projects are sufficiently different from the kinds of investments for which NPV has traditionally been used that it is unwise to apply this technique. On the other hand, the corporation may require an NPV analysis for all capital requests. Under these circumstances, one is in a difficult position of having to use a capital budgeting technique that has significant problems with several types of IT investments.

An NPV Example

In Chapter 8, we discussed how information technology enabled major organizational change at Frito-Lay. The study describing the first part of this initiative, a hand-held computer project for route sales representatives, indicates that management made a decision to fund the project based on a feeling that the benefits would outweigh the costs of the project. To some extent, the company was forced into some kind of a new investment because the existing system involved drivers completing tickets that were scanned. The scanners were wearing out, and the manufacturer had stopped making them.

It is possible to use the numbers in the study (Applegate 1993) and estimates from the managers to conduct a very high level net present value analysis of the investment (see Table 10-1). The initial estimate for the cost of the project was $40 million, which consisted of costs for the hand-held computers, installation in trucks, training, and upgrades in the communications system to transmit the data from each sales district to headquarters in Dallas. The IT staff estimated the new system would increase data center operating costs from $12 million a year to $15 million.

Table 10-1
The Frito-Lay Hand-held Computer Project

Year	0	1	2	3	4	5
Cost (millions)	40	3	3	3	3	3
New Revenue		15	15	15	15	15
Net Cash Flow	−40	12	12	12	12	12
Interest Rate =	10%					
Discount Factor		0.909	0.826	0.751	0.683	0.621
Discounted NCF	−40	10.909	9.917	9.016	8.196	7.451
NPV (5 Yr) =	$5.5					

Table 10-1 is a simple NPV analysis of these data showing the investment cost and increased operating costs each year. The savings figures come from management's estimate that it can increase sales by 10 percent a year through moving to micromarketing and regionalization. The company had sales of almost $3 billion at the time, assuming a 10 percent increase in sales gives $300 million a year. If margins are 10 percent (they are higher on the average), that means $30 million a year in profits. If we arbitrarily assign half of the benefits to the hand-held computer project, that gives $15 million a year in new revenue.

Table 10-1 shows cost and new revenue amounts, and their difference is the net cash flow. We compute and show the discount factor because in many analyses, the net cash flow will be different each year, so it will be necessary to roll back each year's net to the starting point of the analysis. Note how much less a dollar is worth each year further into the future at a 10 percent interest rate.

This high-level analysis shows a positive net present value of $5.5 million, though management evidently proceeded to authorize the investment without this kind of financial analysis. As we saw in Chapter 8, this investment yielded a large number of benefits to Frito-Lay. Later, a manager estimated that the company saved $40 million a year in "stales," products that would have had to be thrown out because they had been on the shelf too long. Clearly, this application had some direct, measurable savings. A rough NPV analysis would have supplemented management's intuitive decision, reduced their uncertainty about the investment, and possibly stimulated more enthusiasm for the project among managers.

A Controversial Approach: The Options Pricing Framework

It is often the case that today's investment in IT makes it possible to undertake a major initiative sometime in the future. For example, American Airlines invested in the SABRE system to solve its immediate problem of making reservations when it introduced jets into its fleet. This initial investment provided the foundation for a travel-related "supermarket" and the deployment of terminals to travel agencies. This first investment led to a subsidiary whose value is almost half the value of AMR Corporation, the parent of American.

An interesting way to think about a current IT investment is that this investment provides you with an option to undertake a project in the future. The initial American reservation system provided an option to develop a host of travel-related services. With these services added to the basic system, American had another option to install terminals in travel agencies. This option is somewhat analogous to the option that one can purchase to buy a stock in the future, known as a call option.

A key insight from this analogy is that *an option does not have to be exercised*. If you have an option to buy shares of stock for $50 a share, and the value of the stock is $45 when the option is to be exercised, you will simply let the option expire. Your only cost is the cost of the option; you are not forced to buy the shares of stock. Similarly, a company may decide not to undertake an IT project it planned when the opportunity comes up to invest in it. Viewing an IT investment using the options framework is particularly appropriate for infrastructure investments; we often invest in infrastructure to enable further applications of technology.

There are two kinds of IT investment situations where the options framework is particularly useful. The first was discussed earlier, in which the firm is deciding whether to make an investment that enables it to undertake another IT initiative in the future. Here, you are analyzing a current and a possible future investment. There can also be a single decision situation where an options framework is helpful. Consider a decision on when, if at all, to undertake a new project. You might be interested in having the option to invest in an IT project one, two, and three years into the future. For both of these situations, different researchers have suggested treating the IT investment as an option and using one of several options pricing models (OPM) for valuing the option. These models originated in the finance literature as ways to value stock options.

An investor buys a stock option to have the opportunity to buy (or sell) shares of a stock at some point in the future. The investor pays the asking price for the option. The option itself is for a specific number of shares. For a call option, the buyer has the right to buy this number of shares at the strike price of the option. If you buy a call option on 100 shares of XYZ stock with a strike price of $50 share, you have the right to exercise this option at its expiration date. If the shares of stock are selling at that date for $55, you will exercise the option, paying $50 for each share and immediately selling it for $55. If the share price is $49, then you would let the option expire.

The most famous pricing model was developed by Black and Scholes (1973); it arrives at a theoretical options price based on the following assumptions:

1. A known and constant interest rate.

2. A stock price following a random walk with a variance proportional to the square of the price.

3. The stock pays no dividends or distributions.

4. The option is exercised only at expiration.

5. There are no transactions costs.

6. One can borrow to purchase or hold at the interest rate in 1.

7. There are no penalties to selling short, i.e., selling without owning the security.

Given these assumptions, the model for the theoretical price of an option is as follows (Black and Scholes 1973):

$$(1) \quad w(x,t) = xN(d_1) - c\, e^{r(t^*-t)}N(d_2)$$

$$(2) \quad d_1 = \frac{\ln(x/c) + (r+0.5\,\sigma^2)(t^* - t)}{\sigma\sqrt{t^* - t}}$$

$$(3) \quad d_2 = \frac{\ln(x/c) + (r - 0.5\,\sigma^2)(t^* - t)}{\sigma\sqrt{t^* - t}}$$

where $w(x,t)$ is the value of an option on stock with price x at time t (for an IT project, w is the value of the project whose underlying risky asset x is the expected revenues from the project); c is the exercise (strike) price (for an IT project, the cost of development); r is the continuously compounded risk-free rate of interest (usually the T-bill rate t^*- t is the duration of the option); σ^2 is the variance of the rate of return or the volatility of the stock (for an IT project, the variance in its expected return); $N(d)$ is the cumulative normal density function.

From a practical standpoint the data required for options pricing models are just as difficult to develop as for an NPV analysis. You have to estimate the variance in the expected return on the IT investment. In the case of an options trader, the variance is the variability of the underlying stock. The options specialist obtains this information from a firm that clears trades; this firm calculates several measures of variance, or volatility, as it is known in options valuation. What is the basis for estimating this variability on a new investment in IT?

The analogy between the call option on a stock and an option on a "real asset" like an IT investment is shown in Table 10-2 (Kumaraswamy 1996).

Table 10-2

Comparison of Stock and IT Project Options

	Call Option on a stock	**Real Option on IT Project**
Underlying asset	Common stock on which option is purchased	An IT system that will be developed in the future
Current value	Current price of stock	Expected present value of returns from the IT project
Volatility	Stock price fluctuations in the market	Uncertainty (variance) in expected cash flow from the IT project
Exercise price	Price in the option at which holder may buy shares when exercising the option	Investment required in IT project
Exercise date	Date on the option when it can be exercised	Date for developing the IT project

For the options trader, the specialist sets the strike prices of the option. For an IT investment, you must estimate the investment required to develop a project at the expiration date of the option, that is, at the time you might be undertaking the project. For an option three years in the future, the analyst has to estimate how much investment would be required. Many variables influence this cost, including the pace of technological change. In three years, a package might come along like SAP that dramatically changes the cost of an investment.

Options pricing models have been used in contexts other than the stock market. For example, companies employ them widely to value stock options for managers and report them to shareholders. It remains to be seen whether the problems with using an OPM for IT investments will be resolved. The framework it offers for viewing certain IT opportunities, however, is very valuable.

This model has a number of advantages, though its application in the context of IT projects is, to say the least, controversial. The advantages include the fact that the model fits the kind of decision problem described earlier; a firm may find itself in a situation, especially with infrastructure expenses, to invest now in order to have the option of undertaking another initiative in the future. The options framework is also useful when a firm is deciding on the timing of an IT investment; it might take an "option" on the initiative at one of several times in the future. The model does take the variability of expected returns, or risk, from the project into account, something that we have stressed in discussions of conversion effectiveness.

Why the controversy? Some experts in finance argue that options pricing models should not be used for nontradable assets. The stocks underlying options trade as do the options themselves. Do IT investments "trade"? What is the value of a partially finished IT project, or what is its salvage value? Is there a market for such projects? In options valuation one can ignore the option's risk because the investor can always hold some quantity of the underlying asset to hedge this risk. The option plus the underlying asset provide a riskless asset's return. As a result, one can price the option from the price of the underlying asset, whose price itself reflects the risk and the investor's risk aversion. If one cannot hedge because there is no traded underlying asset, then the option becomes like any other asset given its risk and return characteristics. An expert in financial options would argue that this asset should be valued as any other, based on its risk and return. The lack of an underlying asset then makes the use of options pricing inappropriate. To overcome the problem of nontraded underlying assets, it is sometimes possible to construct a proxy such as a combination of traded assets. If you wanted to calculate an option on an untraded gold mine, you could use gold futures contracts to proxy the return from the gold mine. In this way you have constructed a proxy in which to invest, an investment that should trade the same way the underlying, nontraded gold mine would trade. Can one construct such a proxy for an IT project? The answer is clearly no, so we are left with a major violation of the option pricing model's underlying assumptions in applying it to IT projects.

In applying models it is not unusual to violate one or more of their assumptions. The issue is whether or not the violation is material; does it lead to incorrect conclusions and results? Unlike the options pricing specialist, the manager confronting an IT investment is not pricing a stock option for purchase or sale. Instead, this manager seeks guidance on making an investment.

It is also possible to conduct an elaborate decision tree and net present value analysis for projects in which there is a second stage or where the decision involves the question of when to make an investment. At some point in the future, there will be a branch in the decision tree if you have the option to either make a further investment or to invest no more in a particular IT project. Unattractive branches drop out of the analysis. The idea is to make the present value computation come closer to reflecting the options that a project presents. This kind of analysis is not likely to produce exactly the same conclusions as an options pricing model, but it does offer an alternative if the OPM seems overly complex or if you are concerned about violating its assumptions.

On balance, used in combination with other information, the options pricing model may provide some insights into the investment decision. I would not recommend making a decision solely "by the numbers" using either NPV or OPM because of (1) the estimates of costs and future returns one is required to make and (2) the fact that neither approach seems to fit precisely the context of IT investment decisions.

OPM Examples

There are three different examples of OPM in the literature; two deal with simple, hypothetical examples, and one uses actual data to explore a decision using the OPM framework that had been made several years earlier.

A Hypothetical Hospital System. The easiest OPM to understand and apply uses the Cox and Rubinstein binomial options pricing model instead of Black Scholes (Kambil, Henderson, and Mohsenzadeh 1993). In this hypothetical example, a hospital is evaluating hand-held computers for use by nurses and physicians. The investment required to undertake this IT initiative totals $4 million, consisting of $1 million in hardware and LAN (local area network) expenses, $2.5 million for the computers and applications programming, and $500,000 for training and implementation.

The task force studying the project identified a number of project risks and then estimated cash flows under different scenarios. In the first scenario, starting in three years, there would be a $1.8 million annual savings from reduced paper-processing costs. The probability of this outcome is 40 percent. The pessimistic scenario resulted in higher costs and lower savings for an annual reduction of $600,000. The probability of the less successful outcome is 60 percent.

Using traditional PV techniques and a 20 percent cost of capital, Kambil, Henderson, and Mohsenzadeh (1993) compute the present value of the optimistic scenario at $6.25 million and the pessimistic scenario at $2.083 million. Weighting these outcomes by their probabilities produces an expected present value of

$$(6.25) \times 0.4 + (2.083) \times 0.6 = \$3.75 \text{ million}$$

The expected net present value is $3.75 million - $4 million, or -$250,000. Following the standard NPV decision rule, the hospital should not undertake the project.

The task force then thought about an alternative; they could fund a pilot project for $1.1 million to develop the LAN along with a limited test of the hand-held computers. If the results turned out to be favorable, then the hospital would undertake the full project. The pilot project would not have positive cash flows, since there would be little savings from a prototype. However, one could look at the pilot as an investment in a real option, the option to undertake the full application if successful. The pilot provides the opportunity, but not an obligation, to invest in the full hand-held project in a year.

A year from the decision to undertake the pilot, management will be better able to assess the outcome from the full project. Earlier, we saw that the expected value of the two scenarios is $6.25 million and $2.083 million. The option is to be exercised a year from now, so we must compute the value of each scenario one year in the future. It is 1 plus the cost of capital to the firm times the present value, or 1.2 times the $6.25 million and $2.083 million figures. These computations give a value from the two outcomes from the pilot of $7.5 million on the optimistic side and $2.5 million for a pessimistic scenario.

The Cox Rubinstein model for the value of an option is:

$$C = \{C_u \, [(r-d)/(u-d)] + C_d[(u-r)/(u-d)]\}/r$$

where C is the current value of the call; C_u is the value of the option at the end of period if the stock price rises to uS; C_d is the value of option t the end of the period if the stock price falls to dS. The underlying model is that there is a stock of asset of current value S. After one period the stock can increase to a value u × S with probability q or decrease to a value d × S with a probability of (1-q). Given an exercise price of K, the value of a call option on this stock is C in the Cox Rubinstein formula. At the end of this period, the value of the option is either max [0, uS - K] with probability q, or max [0,dS - K] with probability 1 - q.

To evaluate this investment from an options pricing perspective, we need to determine values for S, u, and d. S is a twin security that is to match the behavior of the project; it must have a value equal to the expected present value of the original project, $3.75 million. In one year the security S will be worth either $7.5 million under the optimistic outcome or $2.5 million under the pessimistic one. One year from the evaluation, the project is worth either u × S = $7.5 million or d × S = $2.5 million, which means u = 2.0 and d = 0.67.

Solving the Cox Rubinstein equation for the option value C gives $1.18 million. This amount exceeds the present value of the investment required for the pilot, $1.1 million, so from a financial standpoint, the pilot project looks reasonable. Of course, we have violated some assumption of the options pricing model, the most serious being the fact that there is no real twin security S that can track the value of the project. There is no market for the project, and the underlying asset cannot be traded. You can use the OPM to provide additional information for making an IT investment decision, but it should not be the only factor considered. If both the NPV and OPM results were negative, there is a message that the project under consideration is not viewed positively from a capital budgeting standpoint. However, even with this outcome, some other reasons might justify the IT investment. For example, the strategic potential of the proposed IT initiative, or the need to keep up with competitors might convince management to invest.

A Two-Stage Project. Another opportunity to consider the options framework is on two-stage projects, where it is necssary to undertake a first-stage project in order to invest in the second stage (Dos Santos 1991). The second-stage project provides uncertain benefits, especially when trying to make the decision on the first-stage investment. In this situation, it may be necessary to complete the first-stage project before being able to forecast the benefits from a follow-on investment. It is very difficult to estimate these benefits or the probability that they will be realized. Dos Santos (1991) points out that NPV in this situation requires an assumption that the firm will undertake the second-stage project when, in fact, it may not. It also requires the decision maker to enumerate all possible outcomes of the second-stage project along with their value and probability of occurring. The options framework fits the logic of the decision problem. We know the cost of the first-stage project and would like to consider buying an option on the second-stage investment.

One solution is to use an options valuation model developed by Margrabe, which prices an option to exchange one risky asset for another. This model is applied to exchanging risky development costs for risky revenues (Dos Santos 1991). The model requires that the user estimate a large number of parameters, including the current value of the expected benefits of the second-stage project, the current value of its expected development costs, the variance of the rate of change of development costs and the revenues in the second-stage project, and the correlation between development costs and revenues for the follow-on project.

$$V = B_1 N (d_1) - C_1 N (d_2)$$

where V is the value of an option to exchange an asset with an expected value of C_1 (expected investment in the second-stage project) for an asset with expected return of B_1 (expected benefits of second stage project); B_1 is the current value of the expected benefits of a second-stage project; C_1 is the current value of the expected development costs of the second-stage project; and N(d) is the cumulative standard probability density function.
where ln is the natural logarithm function.

$$d_1 = \frac{\ln(B_1/C_1) + \sigma^2 t/2}{\sigma \sqrt{t}}$$

$$d_2 = d_1 - \sigma \sqrt{t}$$

where ln is the natural logarithm function; σ^2 is $(\sigma^2_{B1} + \sigma^2_{C1} - 2 \sigma_{B1}\sigma_{C1}\rho_{BC})$; σ_{B1}^2 is the variance of the rate of change of development costs of the second-stage project; σ^2_{C1} is the variance of the rate of change of revenues of the second-stage project; ρ_{BC} is the correlation between development costs and revenues for the second-stage project; t is the duration of the project.

Dos Santos (1991) presents an example of investing in ISDN service in stage one with a follow-on project dependent on the results of stage one. In the hypothetical example, the numbers come out as expected; NPV is negative, but the options pricing approach suggests the investment is reasonable. The parameters required by this particular model are even more difficult to estimate in the context of an IT investment than Black Scholes or Cox Rubinstein.

Timing an Investment for Yankee 24. The third example of an OPM for IT investments is a post hoc analysis of a decision by a bank network on when and if to enter the debit card business (Benaroch and Kauffman, forthcoming). The network, Yankee 24, had an option to enter the point-of-sale (POS) debit card business at several points over a four-year period. Benaroch and Kauffman interviewed a number of officials involved in making the decision and subsequently implementing the debit card program. One of the most interesting aspects of this project was the ability of the researchers to obtain actual estimates for some of the critical parameters in the model. Probably the most difficult and uncertain estimate is the volatility of expected revenues, which were set at 50 percent based on discussions with Yankee 24 personnel.

This opportunity raises another problem with options pricing models and the IT investment decision. Most of the models deal with European options, options that can be exercised only at one point in time. The Yankee 24 investment decision, as many other IT projects, could really take place at any point of time in the future. Such a timing pattern corresponds to an American option. The researchers used Black's approximation to evaluate the Yankee 24 decision problem, as shown in Table 10-3.

The analysis is based on determining the prices of European options at the latest maturity date (in this case, year 4) and the price of a European option at each maturity date. In Table 10-3 the researchers chose six-month intervals beginning in 1987. The American option price at each date is the maximum of the European option at year 4, or the European option at that date as shown in Table 10-3 in the "Maximum" row.

Table 10-3 shows that the best price is in year 3 from the options pricing analysis, so the financial analysis results in a recommendation to defer the entry into POS debit cards until the beginning of 1990. Looking at the discounted values in the third row of numbers, which is benefits less costs discounted, the maximum value is reached at year 2.5 and there is a dramatic drop at year 3.5. These numbers suggest that a deferral of the investment for two and a half or three years makes sense. The options analysis agrees with this interpretation of the data on discounted costs and benefits.

It is interesting to note that Yankee 24 made the decision to defer its entry into POS services for three years, but without the benefits of the model. The reasons for this deferral included a desire to wait for the uncertainty about consumer acceptance of debit cards to be resolved and the need to wait for Yankee 24's switching capabilities to have enough slack to add POS services. A special report in 1989 also stimulated interest among merchants in the cost advantages of debit cards over other forms of payments. The POS business grew from no debit terminals in 1990 to about 27,000 by early 1993 (Benaroch and Kauffman, forthcoming).

It is interesting to compare the reasons for Yankee 24's entry with the options pricing model recommendations. It appears that the network did not have the capacity to begin debit card services in 1987, so that beginning at that time might not have been possible. While deferring their entry, management was able to gather more information about the likely acceptance of debit card

Table 10-3

Yankee 24 POS Debit Card Investment

t (length of deferral period)	0	0.5	1	1.5
Calendar time	Jan. 87	July 87	Jan. 88	July 88
Black-Scholes Parameter Values				
A_t (A_0 less revenues foregone during waiting)	$323,233	$342,216	$360,083	$376,230
X_t (discounted investment cost, X_0; 3.5 percent interest/ 6 months)	$400,000	$393,179	$386,473	$379,883
$A_t - X_t$	($76,767)	($50,963)	($26,391)	($3,652)
Black's Approximation Results				
C_T (option maturing at time T)				
C_t (option maturing at time t)	$0	$32,024	$66,093	$96,830
Maximum [max(C_T - C_t)]	$65,300	$65,300	$66,093	$96,830
Suggested deferral time (in years)		0.5	1.0	1.5

Assumptions

1. *Transactions volume*—The New England market is 25 percent of the California market, and the POS debit transaction volume expected in New England is estimated based on the experience in California. Until the end of 1991 the total number of POS debit transactions in California was around 12 million, and by the end of 1992 the number of transactions per month rose to 10 million. These figures imply a 16 percent per month growth rate in transaction volume in California between 1985 and 1992. This growth rate is consistent with expert estimates of the growth rate expected between 1993 and 1996. Assuming that the New England and California markets are similar, except for size, we applied a similar growth rate. (A similar estimate would have been established based on the transaction volume in California between 1985 and 1987.) A base of 2.5 million transactions for December 1992 is used, based on a corresponding 10 million figure in California. The base figure is discounted back by the 16 percent growth rate per month, and the monthly transaction volumes are aggregated by year.

2. A—the present value of revenues less operational costs, where the discount rate of 12 percent approximates the rate used for capital budgeting of other electronic banking investments at the time. The yearly operational marketing cost is $40,000 ($20,000 every six months), and the revenue per transaction is 10¢. Once an entry decision is made, it takes one year to begin servicing customers.

3. X—initial (sunk) technical investment is $400,000.

4. s—volatility of expected revenues is 50 percent.

5. T—the maximum deferral period in years, from (early) 1987 to (early) 1992, is also the analysis horizon of 5.5 years.

r_f—7 percent annual risk-free interest rate.

2	2.5	3	3.5	4
Jan. 89	**July 89**	**Jan. 90**	**July 90**	**Jan.91**
$389,207	$395,566	$387,166	$344,813	$223,295
$373,404	$367,036	$360,777	$354,625	$348,577
$15,803	$28,530	$26,389	($9,812)	($125,281)
				$65,300
$123,786	$144,565	$152,955	$134,873	$65,300
$123,786	$144,565	$152,955	$134,873	$65,300
2.0	2.5	3.0	3.5	4.0

Year-Month	Number of Transactions	Operational		
		Revenues	Costs	Cash Flows
Jan.87	0	$0	$0	$0
July 87	0	$0	$0	$0
Jan.88	3,532	$353	$20,000	($19,647)
July 88	8,606	$861	$20,000	($19,139)
Jan.89	20,969	$2,097	$20,000	($17,903)
July 89	51,088	$5,109	$20,000	($14,891)
Jan.90	124,470	$12,447	$20,000	($7,553)
July 90	303,258	$30,326	$20,000	$10,326
Jan.91	738,857	$73,886	$20,000	$53,886
July 91	1,800,149	$180,015	$20,000	$160,015
Jan.92	4,385,877	$438,588	$20,000	$418,588

services. Neither the qualitative or OPM analysis could have foreseen the critical industry report that stimulated merchant demand for POS service.

Guidelines for IT Investments

Table 10-4 lists suggested guidelines for evaluating IT investments based on the type of application being undertaken. Infrastructure investment offers a good opportunity for evaluation using an options framework. A significant portion of infrastructure exists to provide a platform for other applications. A LAN alone is not very interesting without workstations and office software; custom applications using the LAN create value from this infrastructure investment. At the time management makes the decision to commit funds to the LAN, it may not know exactly what these future opportunities will be. The upside of this investment is the new initiatives it allows.

In some instances, you will have to invest in infrastructure to make possible an application in some other category. Frito-Lay had to develop a VSAT satellite network to communicate data from drivers' hand-held computers back to headquarters. This infrastructure expense was a part of the total hand-held computer project and was included in its justification.

For investments that are required, there is unlikely to be a great deal of upside; conceptually it is easiest to view these investments as a cost of doing business. Most firms will look for the lowest-cost way to get the required features, with the first choice being an applications package. You want to implement required applications quickly and for as little cost as possible.

For investments where technology is the only way to do the job, the main question is whether or not you have to perform the task. If the answer is yes, then it is worth spending time thinking about the upside potential. Might the investment lead to major cost savings? Are there opportunities for generating a stream of revenue? The options pricing framework can provide information here if you are able to make reasonable estimates for the parameters in the models.

Investments where one expects to see a direct return are natural candidates for net present value analysis. This kind of application is the textbook case for using discounted cash flows for the capital budgeting decision.

Where the potential for indirect returns exists, the decision maker will have to rely heavily on estimates and a qualitative evaluation of the possible upside from the investment. The options view is helpful here even if used just as a framework for understanding the costs and possible future benefits. If you can prepare estimates with confidence, then an OPM will provide additional information for making an investment decision.

Table 10-4

Investment Opportunities Matrix and Evaluation Strategy

Type of Investment	Comments	Upside	Probability of return	Evaluation Approach
Infra-structure	Support current business (may allow for future investments)	Little itself, but allows new initiatives	0.2 to 1.0 (0.5)	1. General infra-structure: Look at it as an option for future applications 2. For a current initiative in another category: part of its investment cost
Required (no return) Managerial control	A cost of doing business	Almost none	0 to 0.5 (0.2)	Look for the low-est-cost way to get the required features of the application (probably a package)
No other way to do the job	Enable new task or process, provide better customer service	Could gain more than forecast	0.5 to 1.0 (0.75)	Can look at cost minimization and/or estimate upside and look at investment in options framework
Direct return from IT	Structured, cost/benefit, and NPV appropriate	A little if you can build on the investment	0.7 to 1.0 (0.9)	Net present value, possibly options pricing model
Indirect returns	Potential for considerable return, but indirect benefits hard to estimate	Could be substantial future benefits	0 to 1.0 (0.5)	View in an options framework

continued on next page

Table 10-4
continued from previous page

Type of Investment	Comments	Upside	Probability of return	Evaluation Approach
Competitive necessity	Need the system to compete in the business; what is the cost of not investing in technology?	Very little if you are following the industry	0 to 1.0 (0.2)	Have to match features of competitors; little choice here but to invest or cede the business; match value of business to cost
Strategic application	High risk-high potential; may be able to estimate return only after implementation	A high potential	0 to 1.0 (0.5)	Investing now for possible large future gain; the options framework may apply
Transformational IT	Must be combined with changes in management philosophy; good for fast response organization (risky to change structure, but high potential rewards)	A high potential	0 to 1.0 (0.5)	Potential for future gain, but likely a part of a management change program

Initiatives in the competitive necessity category involve balancing the cost of the investment against the value of the line of business. If management judges the initiative to be a requirement to maintain market share, it can compare that cost against the cost of lost market share. An NPV analysis is possible, though simply comparing the cost/loss ratio may be enough. As an example, there is one software vendor that is discontinuing supporting its application because of the year 2000 problem. Fixing the problem is a requirement for staying in business. While the cost of the actual fix is not great in this case, the potential liability for an error is higher than the value of the business.

Strategic applications have a high risk, and their payoff may not be clear until well after management makes an investment in them. This type of investment looks suited to the options framework, since the revenue or cost savings stream is likely to be in the future and is highly uncertain.

Transformational IT will be a part of a larger management change program. At Oticon, the chairman needed new information technology to implement his change program, to transform Oticon into a "spaghetti" organization. The company's performance has improved, but it is very difficult to claim that IT deserves credit for the financial results. It is most likely that management will evaluate transformational IT as a cost component of an entire change program without trying to tie back gains from the transformation to specific parts of the program.

Information for IT Investment Decisions

Table 10-5 presents information for making decisions about IT investments. This spreadsheet combines information from the Investment Opportunities Matrix in Chapter 1, the IT Investment Equation and the IT Value Equation from Chapter 2, and capital budgeting techniques discussed in this chapter. Thinking back to Chapter 2, the IT Investment Equation states that the likelihood of a return on an IT investment is not 100 percent. Instead, there is a probability of a return given the type of investment and a probability of conversion success in turning an investment into a working application. The product of these two probabilities gives the S/R index or the probability of a successful return. Restating the IT Investment Equation:

$$P(\text{Success/Return}) = P(\text{Return on Investment Type}) \times P(\text{Conversion Success})$$

The intuition behind the S/R index is that there is less than a 100 percent chance of a return on most IT investments, and less than a 100 percent chance of conversion success. Combining these two chances into the S/R index provides a more realistic view of the likely return from an IT investment.

Most of the time those proposing an IT initiative and managers evaluating proposals want to know the expected return from the investment. By multiplying the S/R index by the estimate of the project's return, we obtain an expected return that is weighted by the two above-mentioned chances or probabilities. The IT Value Equation restated is:

$$
\begin{aligned}
\text{Expected Return} &= \text{Estimated Return} \times P(\text{Return}) \times P(\text{Conversion Success}) \text{ or} \\
&= \text{Estimated Return} \times P(\text{Success/Return}) \text{ or} \\
&= \text{Estimated return} \times \text{IT Investment Equation}
\end{aligned}
$$

Table 10-5 is an example of the information that management could use in making IT investment decisions. I do not advocate that any one decision criterion determines the investment decision except in rare circumstances; management needs to look at all aspects of the decision. The table identifies each IT initiative in this hypothetical example and lists its type. (One initiative might fit in more than one type, which makes for a slightly more complicated analysis; however, the same approach applies.) The fourth column of the table is an estimated return from the project. The next two columns are probability estimates, the first being the probability that this project, given its type, will have a return. The second probability is for conversion effectiveness. What is the risk of this initiative? How likely is it that the organization can implement it successfully to meet specifications?

The S/R index comes from the IT Investment Equation: It is the product of the probability of a return and the probability of successful conversion and represents the likelihood of a successful return. The expected value comes from the IT Value Equation; it is the estimated return times the probability of a return times the probability of conversion (or the estimated return times the S/R index).

The Capital Budget Model column contains the results of applying a budgeting technique to the data in the table. Note that these techniques do not necessarily apply in every instance. The right-most column in Table 10-5 comments on the possible upside benefits of the investment.

Table 10-5 contains a variety of projects for a rather diversified, hypothetical holding company. The company convenes an IT steering committee as needed; one of its tasks is to approve suggested projects. One can look at present IT investments from the budgeting system to Web home pages and the proposed IT investment for an Intranet shown in Table 10-5 as a portfolio of IT projects. Management should try to balance this portfolio on several criteria. For example, it is unlikely that one will obtain great value if all conversion probabilities are very low, or if all expected values are small. The S/R index provides an overall evaluation of the opportunity to create value from IT. Comparing a proposed project with the existing portfolio provides a picture of its contribution to the firm's efforts to obtain value from IT.

In the past, the steering committee made decisions on all of the projects in Table 10-5 except the last one, the proposed Intranet. A review of its past decisions will set the stage for discussing the new initiative for an Intranet.

The budgeting system falls into the "required" category of application. Both the company's accounting firm and its controller argued strongly that the

Table 10-5

A Decision Worksheet

Name	Type	Cost	Estimated Return	Prob Return	Prob Conv	Prob S/R	Expected Value	Capital Budget Model	Upside
Budgeting system	Required	$20,000	$20,000	0.50	1.00	0.50	$10,000	$	None
JIT/EDI system	Direct	300,000	500,000	1.00	0.75	0.75	375,000	957,058	Expand $5 million savings
Infra-structure network	Infra-structure	100,000	75,000	0.60	0.80	0.48	36,000	120,678	Allow future applications
Delivery tracking	Competi-tive necessity	750,000	1,000,000	0.40	1.00	0.40	400,000		Prevent market share loss
Groupware	Indirect	100,000	50,000	0.90	0.80	0.72	36,000		Restructure firm?
Web order entry	Direct	100,000	500,000	0.90	0.70	0.63	315,000	1,055,929	Reduce cost $500,000
Web home pages	Com-petitive	50,000	—	0.00	1.00	0.00	—		Experience for e-commerce
Proposed Intranet	Infra-structure	160,000	60,000	0.80	0.90	0.72	43,200		Internal Intranet
								144,813	Present value 5 yrs savings
								(15,187)	NPV original proposal
								37,608	Options Price experiment

old budgeting system was no longer suitable. The cost of this system is rather low, as the company identified a package for $10,000; it estimated that no more than another $10,000 would be required to implement the package. The controller estimated an annual savings of $20,000 in reduced clerical costs once the package is implemented. However, she lacked confidence in her estimate given this type of investment and the required nature of the application; she estimates a 50 percent probability of a return. The IT staff was very confident that it could install the system successfully; they rate the probability of conversion success as 1. The steering committee approved the system because its cost was low and because the controller made a strong argument that such a system was required for the business.

The JIT/EDI system for one of the company's manufacturing subsidiaries required lengthy discussion due to the size of the investment. Based on visits to other companies using this approach, including Chrysler, the IT staff felt that their company could expect to get all of the estimated returns (probability of a return = 1.0); they also estimated a 75 percent probability of successful conversion. Given a project with an expected annual value then of $375,000 ($500,000 × 1.0 × 0.75) and a $300,000 investment, there was no question about the economics of the proposal. The Capital Budget column shows a PV of a little under $1 million using a five-year planning horizon and a 15 percent cost of capital; the NPV is $957,058 - 300,000, or $657,058. The major issue for the steering committee was the $300,000 investment and the demands this system would place on the IT staff. A system of this size, done in-house, might preclude some other IT initiatives, or force the firm to go outside for them. The steering committee approved this proposal because of its favorable financial projections and the upside possibility of even larger savings from expanding the system in the future.

The third project originated in two departments of a subsidiary; it is an infrastructure investment for a local area network linking the two departments, with connections to the Internet. The estimated cost is $100,000, and the expected annual value of the return is $36,000. This expected value comes from the product of a 0.6 probability of an estimated $75,000 return and a 0.8 probability of conversion success. The five-year NPV of a $36,000 annual savings at the firm's cost of capital is $120,678 - $100,00, or a positive $20,678. However, the steering committee decided against funding this proposal despite the positive economic evaluation. Instead, it asked the departments proposing the LAN to work with their IT group to propose a network for the whole subsidiary rather than just two departments.

A competitor recently began tracking all of its products using scanners in its trucks and bar codes on all packages. The trucks return to their base each night and transmit their data to a central computer where customers can make inquiries about the status of their shipments. Company management proposed a similar system to remain competitive. Because the firm felt that technology vendors have a lot of experience with this kind of application, it estimated the probability of conversion as 1.0. The $1 million in estimated annual returns was a figure that inspired little confidence; weighting it by a probability of a return of .40 gives an expected value for the project of $400,000. The estimated return was based on the vice president of marketing's estimate of lost market share if the company did not make this investment. Given the uncertainty on the benefits side, the IT staff did not feel comfortable applying a capital budgeting model. The IT steering committee approved the project based on the argument that package tracking had become a competitive necessity, and because it wanted to help this subsidiary grow.

Another subsidiary requested funding for a groupware initiative, a project that at best would have only indirect benefits. Arguments in favor of the investment stressed the opportunities groupware offered to restructure the organization. This subsidiary has a large, mobile staff of representatives who call on customers and make proposals to them. Groupware would reduce the cycle time for proposals and allow the company to decentralize more decision making to its representatives. Senior management felt that such IT support would help the subsidiary compete by providing a fast response to customers. Management admitted that its return estimate was a guess, so the steering committee looked at the project from the standpoint of its potential upside benefits for the subsidiary.

The proposal for a Web order entry application was an easy one to approve. The NPV was $1,056 million - $100,000, or $956,000 for five years at a 15 percent cost of capital. However, the steering committee was less concerned with the economic analysis than with the future; it sees the Internet as an important sales channel for many parts of the company. It was eager to see the first direct ordering initiative on the Web, and quickly approved the request.

Similarly, a subsidiary wanted to establish a home page and related pages on the Web. It argued for the investment, not on a return basis, but because its competitors already had Web sites. It viewed the proposal as a first step in moving toward electronic commerce. Since the steering committee had a policy promoting the use of the Internet, it approved this proposal as well.

The proposed Intranet looks very attractive compared to the projects already underway or completed. It has a high S/R index with a good probability of conversion success and of obtaining a return. The subsidiary requesting the Intranet classified it as an infrastructure expense. The subsidiary would gain from making information available throughout its operations, and estimated that it could save $60,000 a year in paper and publishing costs. The NPV analysis shows a five-year value of $144,813 using a 15 percent cost of capital; the NPV is this amount less $160,000, or -$15,187. The NPV in this case is negative.

The subsidiary then recast its analysis of the Intranet in an options pricing model. First the analyst determined that the company could develop a prototype for $30,000. This test Intranet would give enough information to know if the original proposal should be undertaken. At the end of the proto-type development in a year, the company would need to invest another $100,000 to develop the full Intranet. She examined the $60,000 in estimated benefits and saw that this amount could be viewed as the combination of an optimistic scenario of $80,000, occurring with a probability of 0.6, and a pes-simistic scenario of $30,000, having a probability of 0.4. Weighting each of these outcomes by the S/R probability index of 0.72, she computed the value of the option the company would "buy" if it undertook the prototype. The value of the twin security representing the option is $144,813, the NPV of the two benefits scenarios. As in our earlier example, to compute the parameters of the options pricing model, the analyst looked at the future value of the scenar-ios in one year. The final results shown in Table 10-5 indicate the value of the option as $37,608, which is more than its cost of $30,000.

Given this additional information from the OPM, it is likely manage-ment will approve at least the prototype Intranet. With the small amount of money at risk, the firm might decide to proceed with the full project because the evidence for benefits from Intranets in general is very positive. In addition, the steering committee has been very supportive of Internet-type initiatives.

Making Decisions and Monitoring the Portfolio

Decisions about investments in information technology are too important to be left to technologists! For major commitments to new IT initiatives, senior man-agement of the firm needs to be involved in the decision. These managers should follow and monitor the progress of projects, providing advice and resources when there are problems. The kinds of applications we have discussed so far are critical to the firm; they have the potential to return enormous value and the potential to fail miserably. Some of these initiatives protect or even expand market share, whereas others become intertwined with corporate strat-egy. By joining discussions and reviews of IT initiatives, the CEO communicates that these investments are important, encouraging users and managers at all levels to contribute to a project's success.

These examples have shown that different criteria apply to project approval depending on the type of investment. In some cases quantitative analysis is very appropriate; in others decision makers responded to qualitative factors. In surveying different companies about their actual practice in making IT investment decisions, I encountered a group of utilities that insisted on a positive net present value before undertaking any IT project. While this rule probably sounds good to management and shareholders, Table 10-5 suggests that these companies may be missing a lot of opportunities (at least if they are being honest in their NPV analysis).

If a firm insists on a cost benefit, NPV, or even options pricing analysis, it is likely to ignore proposed investments in several of our categories and some opportunities with considerable upside potential. In particular, it is hard to come up with credible quantitative evaluations of infrastructure, initiatives with indirect returns, strategic applications, and investments that may transform the organization. I believe that every proposal should be evaluated, but that decision makers have to use criteria that are appropriate for the type of investment proposed.

Decision-making Summary

Two of this book's objectives are to demonstrate that information technology can produce value for an organization and to describe how management can evaluate IT investment opportunities. This chapter is devoted to the evaluation question. We have seen that IT value varies by the type of investment being considered. In some cases it is relatively easy to estimate returns and their associated probabilities. In these instances we can apply capital budgeting models to provide more economic information about the investment.

In other cases, one does not have to resort to models because of the nature of the application. For example, in a competitive situation the choice may very well be to undertake the initiative or give up market share or even a line of business. The issue is likely to go far beyond the investment in IT to questions of firm strategy and long-term plans. The spreadsheet in Table 10-5 is intended to summarize information for decision making, to support managers charged with the responsibility for allocating scarce IT investment resources to proposed initiatives.

The approach described here, and the arguments in this book, differ from conventional recommendations on investment. The key difference is the observation that there are different types of IT investments, and that we should not expect all of them to show an immediate, quantifiable return. Given this fact, managers have to consider a variety of indicators and factors in making a decision on IT investments. As a result, managers will approve or disapprove different investments on different criteria; there will not be a consistent set of factors that determine whether management funds a project. While this predicament may be uncomfortable for some, we should remember Emerson's 1841 comment:

> A foolish consistency is the hobgoblin of little minds....
> With consistency, a great soul has simply nothing to do.

The challenges of deciding on investments in information technology, given the variety of ways in which technology contributes value to the organization, provide much needed work for a variety of users, IT staff members, and managers.

Some Implications

M anagement determines the value received from investment in information technology. By and large, management gets the kind of information technology it deserves! Chapter 11 offers guidelines for IT management in general and relates them to the IT investment decision. The last chapter summarizes the evidence and techniques suggested in this book. It argues that there is value from investing in information technology, but that the value cannot always be demonstrated through a quantitative analysis of return on investment. Because of this characteristic of IT investment, managers have to be creative in finding value. I am convinced that information technology does provide value, and that managers who view technology as an asset and actively manage it will make a major contribution to the success of their organizations.

CHAPTER ELEVEN

Implications for Managing Information Technology

he basic premise of this book is that information technology can and does produce value for the organization. Firms rarely reduce their stock of technology; they continually add new applications. Occasionally an organization replaces and updates existing applications, but in general the amount of technology in firms is constantly increasing. While an estimated 50 percent of capital spending in the United States is for technology, the total stock of IT is estimated at about 2 percent to 5 percent of all assets. If you add the cost of software, telecommunications, and other office equipment, the total gets to almost 12 percent of assets (Gibbs 1997). Many of the companies discussed in this book find technology to be a pervasive element in their operations. Firms like VeriFone, Calyx and Corolla, Chrysler, and many others depend on the technology to operate.

We have tried to make the case that IT does have a value for the organization. In Chapter 10 we suggested an approach to making information technology investment decisions. The success of investments, even if you make good decisions, depends on the ability of the organization to manage information technology. This capability begins with senior management in the firm, and extends through the entire organization. In this chapter we explore the role of management in obtaining value from IT investments. We shall see that this role is an active one that includes strategy and programs to guide the firm's investment in IT.

There are many different ways to manage the IT effort in a firm. One description focuses on politics; its developers argue that information politics is what determines how successfully the firm applies information technology. Table 11-1 describes the political model (Davenport, Eccles, and Prusak 1992).

Table 11-1

Political Models of IT Management

Technocratic utopianism	Reliance on technology; model the firm's IT structure and rely on new technology
Anarchy	No overall information management
Feudalism	Management of IT by individual business units; limited corporate reporting
Monarchy	Strong control by senior management; information may not be shared with lower levels of the firm
Federalism	Management through consensus and negotiation about key IT decisions and structures

Firms that practice technocratic utopianism are fascinated with the technology. There is an assumption in the firm that technology will solve all problems. The firm will develop databases, desktop workstations, and networks, and purchase large amounts of software. This organization lacks a vision of how all of this technology will be used to further its objectives.

Anarchy results when technology is not managed. Management abrogates its responsibilities to control IT and lets a thousand flowers bloom. This strategy may encourage the bold to acquire computers and connect them, but as the firm matures, the lack of overall planning and standards will create tremendous problems. Many firms practiced this style of management in the early days of PCs, letting users purchase whatever equipment they pleased. As a result, these firms found it very difficult and expensive to connect all of their diverse computers to a network.

In the feudal model, powerful executives control technology within their divisions and departments. These executives determine what information to collect and choose the technology for their fiefdoms. They also make the decision on what information to forward to higher levels of management. This model is most often found when the firm stresses divisional autonomy. Because it is unlikely two chiefs will follow the same model, it again can be very difficult to coordinate different feudal systems if senior management decides that is a more appropriate technology strategy.

In a monarchy, the CIO becomes the CIC, the chief information czar. Instead of playing the consultant role, the CIO establishes and enforces standards that will be followed throughout the corporation. The monarchy often emerges when the firm finds that it has suffered too long from the feudal model. A possible halfway point between feudalism and a monarchy is a constitutional monarchy, in which a document sets out the powers reserved to senior management and those that fall to the divisions.

In today's environment, the federal model may be the most appropriate. The firm tries to reach a consensus on what IT decisions belong at each level and how information should be shared. The emphasis is on what policies make the most sense for the corporation as a whole, not just for a specific department or division. Senior management recognizes that local divisions need some autonomy, and local managers recognize that information belongs to the company and may often be of great strategic value.

The Chief Information Officer

The increased importance of IT to the firm has led to the creation of a chief information officer (CIO) position. This individual is, of course, in charge of information technology in the firm. However, the chief information officer is also an influential member of senior management and is usually a vice president or senior vice president in the firm. In addition to traditional information processing, this individual is responsible for voice and data communications and office technology. The job demands someone who can assume a role in planning, influencing other senior managers, and organizing information activities in the organization.

The CIO must worry about strategic planning for the corporation and how information technology can provide a competitive edge. The executive in this role must provide leadership and control over processing. It is important that planning, systems development, and operations are all undertaken successfully.

The CIO is a relatively new position in organizations, but we expect that more and more firms will create such a post. It is not unusual for a large firm to spend more than $100 million a year on information technology. A manager, not a technician, is needed to obtain a return from this kind of investment.

Earl and Feeny (1994) describe ways in which CIOs should try to add value to their organizations. They found two types of CEOs, those who see IT as a strategic resource and those who see it as a cost. Table 11-2 presents various issues in managing IT as seen by CEOs in these different positions.

Table 11-2

Perceptions of IT

Issue	IT a Cost/Liability	IT an Asset
Are we getting value for money invested in IT?	ROI on IT is difficult to measure; the organization as a whole is unhappy with IT	ROI is difficult to measure; the organization believes IT makes an important contribution
How important is IT?	Stories of strategic IT use are dismissed as irrelevant to this business	Stories of strategic IT use are instructive
How do we plan for IT?	IT plans are made by specialists or missionary zealots	IT thinking is subsumed within business thinking
Is the IS function doing a good job?	There is general cynicism about the track record of IS	The performance of IS is no longer an agenda item
What is the IT strategy?	Many IT applications are under development	IS efforts are focused on a few key initiatives
What is the CEO's vision for the role of IT?	The CEO sees a limited role for IT within the business	The CEO sees IT as having a role in the transformation of the business
What do we expect of the CIO?	The CIO is positioned as a specialist functional manager	The CIO is valued as a contributor to business thinking and business operations

If you are the CIO of a firm whose CEO holds the views in the middle, liability column, then the job will indeed be challenging. Earl and Feeny (1994) argue that the CIO must find a way to add value to the corporation from its use of IT so the CEO will view IT as an asset. Senior management cannot delegate responsibility for IT to the CIO and then ignore him or her. Successful IT management is a major part of obtaining a return from IT investments, and success here requires a team effort involving the CIO and all of top management.

One role of the CIO is to determine if success stories from other industries or from competitors are relevant to the company. In one chemical company, managers dismissed stories of competitive advantage from IT saying they were not applicable in their industry. Unfortunately, at the same time a competitor was developing technology that gave it a competitive advantage.

It appears the most successful approach to obtaining benefits from IT is not to identify separate IT and business strategies; instead business strategy subsumes IT strategy. The job of the CIO is to build relationships with other functional managers so IT requirements become a part of business strategy. This approach means the CIO has to be involved in planning and strategy meetings across the company.

To provide confidence in technology, the CIO must build a track record of delivering IT as promised, on time and within budget. Users quickly become cynical when delivery dates, cost estimates, and functional specifications do not meet expectations. Conversion effectiveness is a major concern for the CIO.

Rather than scattering the development effort, a well-run company focuses its IT efforts on opportunities and areas where the firm is weak. The task of the CIO here is to determine not how to use IT, but rather where it should be used to most benefit the organization. We offered suggestions on selecting IT investments in Chapter 10.

The CIO has to be a promoter who markets the potential of IT to transform the organization. A track record of delivering what has been promised will increase this manager's credibility, as will good examples of organizations that have undergone technology-driven transformations.

Table 11-3 summarizes the characteristics Earl and Feeny (1994) found among CIOs for firms that considered IT to be an asset rather than a liability. This table shows how the CIO can add value to the organization. *From our standpoint, a key role for the CIO is presenting alternatives for investing in IT and the information to support the decision to invest. To complete the investment process, the CIO must see that an IT initiative is completed successfully.*

The CIO of Time Warner spoke recently at New York University about his role in the company, and his comments provided further insights on adding value. According to this CIO, he adds value by finding new business opportunities for the company and using technology to conduct business in new ways. The company manages IT in a federal structure, so he takes responsibility for infrastructure like a worldwide network. IT managers in each division develop systems for their divisions and worry about the day-to-day operation of their

Table 11-3

The Added Value of the CIO

---

1. Obsessive and continuous focus on business imperatives
2. Interpretation of external IT success stories as potential models for the firm
3. Establishment and maintenance of IS executive relationships
4. Establishment and communication of IS performance record
5. Concentration of the IS development effort
6. Achievement of a shared and challenging vision of the role of IT

---

systems. The role of the CIO will differ among companies, but first and foremost this person has to be a manager concerned with the business as well as someone who understands information technology.

A Vision and Plan for IT

One task of a CIO is to be sure there is a vision in the firm for what IT can accomplish and a plan to provide a guideline for management decisions about technology. A vision is a general statement of what the organization is trying to become. A vision describes, possibly in scenario form, the environment seen by a user. For example, "We will use information technology to support our strategies of providing the best customer service in the industry and becoming a global firm. Our first priority is to develop electronic links with customers and suppliers. Next, product brand managers will be furnished with a client workstation that can access the sales database. They will be provided with decision support tools to conduct their own analyses of global data. Product development engineers will have workstations capable of running the CAD/CAM software; we will strive to connect design centers around the world so that they can share each other's work." A vision might include a statement about the kind of technology architecture the firm hopes to provide, say, a client-server environment and a global network for communications. The vision needs to be sufficiently compelling so it creates enthusiasm for the plan to achieve it.

It is important for IT strategy to be subsumed as a part of overall business strategy. Corporate and IT strategic planning should be part of one planning effort. The IT plan expands the IT component of the strategic business plan and describes how to execute the agreed upon strategy. This plan must combine the vision of IT with strategy to produce a document that guides IT decision making. Suppose the overall strategy of the company is to become the low-cost producer in its industry. This strategy is to be achieved by reengineering existing processes and installing automated production equipment in manufacturing plants. The vision of the firm in five years is to have process owners in charge of business processes that have extensive technology support. The overall architecture is client-server, with a network connecting all plants and office locations. In addition, to pursue its low-cost producer strategy, the company will establish electronic links with key customers and suppliers.

Thus, the vision and strategy provide the goals for an IT plan that describes how to achieve them. This more operational plan will depend on the company and its strategy, but in general it will discuss hardware and software, communications, and individual applications. Continuing the above-mentioned example, the plan details the equipment needed to move toward the client-server model and a schedule for implementation. This section would also discuss networking, including the hardware and services required to provide communications.

A key role of the plan is to identify the most important new applications of technology and prioritize them. It is important to focus efforts on applications that contribute to achieving the vision and strategy of the company. For the earlier example, do not be too concerned about routine applications. Management will probably decide resources should be applied to one or two major projects and an effort to develop EDI with customers and suppliers. The plan would describe each of these projects in some detail, including cost, time, and staff requirements for completion. If management decides it wants to undertake more applications than there is staff available, some of the development will have to be outsourced.

Having a plan makes managing IT requests easier for the CIO and for management in general. The rapid diffusion of technology has led to a flood of ideas and requests for how to use IT. The typical organization cannot afford to undertake every application suggested. A manager can evaluate applications against the plan. Does this suggestion help us achieve our vision and strategy? Where does it fall given the priorities of our other projects? In the previous chapter we saw a steering committee relying on policy and the direction of the firm in evaluating some investments. For example, the steering committee wanted to encourage Internet initiatives. Such a focus comes from a plan that should have a major influence on the IT investment decision and portfolio of applications.

A well-prepared plan can create enthusiasm for IT, focus the technology effort on business imperatives as suggested earlier, and help manage and evaluate technology. The plan is a fundamental management tool for seeing that IT makes the maximum contribution to the organization.

I recommend that a representative group of managers work together to develop a plan for information technology and the organization. A plan developed by a CIO alone will probably not be acceptable to other managers. The CIO should act as a resource, consultant, and tutor for the planning committee. The idea is for technology not to be a separate plan, but to be integrated with a corporate plan.

Summary of Issues in Managing IT

The most important issues in managing IT to obtain maximum value from the organization's investment in IT include the following recommendations:

> Senior managers should be involved in making decisions about technology given the huge investments most companies have made and continue to make in information technology.

> You can use information technology to transform the organization. IT design variables let you develop entirely new structures like the ones discussed in Chapter 8.

> Information technology should be an integral part of a firm's corporate strategy. Managers and other users are the most likely source of strategic applications of the technology.

> Senior management needs a vision of how technology can be used in the firm.

> A corporate plan should include planning for IT.

> Management has the responsibility for designing and managing an IT architecture. It has to provide the basic infrastructure needed to take advantage of technology.

> There are a number of different structures for managing IT. Today the federal structure is probably the most popular in a large organization.

> Management is also responsible for developing new applications of technology. It needs to focus development resources where they are most needed.

> Systems development is one of the most creative activities in modern organizations. Managing development projects has been a continuing challenge for companies.

> Management must decide on the source of IT services, for example, there is the option of outsourcing to a consulting firm.

Managers determine what level of support to provide users working with technology, and how much time users should spend developing applications themselves.

Managers are in the business of change. No place is change more evident than in implementing new technology and using IT to redesign organizations.

Information technology, while easy to use in some respects, is constantly growing more complex. There is a continuing need for IT professionals in the organization.

There are a variety of ways in which IT can provide value for the firm; the key to unlocking this value is with management.

The Changing World of Information

The percentage of IT expenditures controlled by the professional IS group has dropped steadily. A corporate IT group is likely to be responsible for "legacy" systems (older systems, often for mainframes), corporate-wide applications, and infrastructure technology, such as networks. More and more, the responsibility for IT management is shifting to users and line managers.

The challenge for senior management in this changing world is to exert the proper amount of influence and oversight of an increasingly complex technological environment. The hardware and software infrastructure is expanding rapidly, as networks of servers and workstations grow. Morgan Stanley has 15,000 computers, and NationsBank has more computers than employees. It is difficult to keep track of, much less manage, all of the software and applications local units develop for their own benefit.

Senior management will continue to struggle with the balance between what appears to be critical for the organization and should be controlled centrally, and what is best left to local management. The trends that are likely to continue are the declining cost of hardware, the explosive growth of networking, the Internet, interorganizational communications, the development of more sophisticated software packages, and the desire of users to do more computing under their own control.

This rapid decentralization means that there will be pressure for separate IT investment budgets for different business units. Senior management has to decide how much coordination among decentralized groups is necessary for the benefit of the organization as a whole. The federal model applies to the decision to invest in IT as it does to other IT management issues.

An Action Plan

It is very difficult to reduce suggestions for managing something as complex as information technology to a few outline points. However, the following suggestions have proven helpful as guidelines for managing IT:

1. Use IT design variables to structure the organization.

   One of the most exciting attributes of modern technology is your ability to use it in designing innovative and highly effective organizations. You can use this technology to design components of an organization, or to structure an entirely new type of organization.

   • IT design variables, in conjunction with conventional organization design variables, provide you with tremendous flexibility in designing an organization.

   • The most likely outcome from using these variables will be a flat organization structure with decentralized decision making. The firm will use electronic communications and linking and electronic customer supplier relationships to form alliances with other firms and in general will resemble the T-Form organization described earlier.

2. Determine and communicate corporate strategy.

   If you and others in the organization are to help the firm achieve its strategy, you must know what it is!

   Develop a plan for how to use information technology. The plan should include the following:

   • A list of opportunities for your business unit.

   • A vision of how your unit should function and the role of IT in that vision.

   • A survey of current business processes that are good candidates for major improvement through new IT initiatives.

3. Develop a long-range plan for the technological infrastructure.

- Plan for hardware/software architecture for your unit given the constraints of the corporation, including technology that already exists.

- Plan for the evolution of a network that forms the backbone of your technology.

- Be willing to invest in infrastructure.

- Investigate the use of standards to facilitate connection and interorganizational systems.

4. Develop an approach to making IT investment decisions.

- Recognize that there are different kinds of IT investments and that they have different returns.

- Develop a structure for making IT investment decisions, for example, a steering committee.

- Provide the kind of information described in Chapter 10 to those making IT investment decisions.

5. Develop ongoing management strategies for IT.

- Support users in your unit and encourage them to work with the technology.

- Develop mechanisms for allocating resources to IT.

- Encourage innovation and reward it.

6. Manage systems development.

- See that design teams are formed for new projects.

- Participate in the design process.

- Be sure you understand what IT applications will do.

- Review and monitor development projects.

7. Be a user of technology.

- Use IT to improve your own productivity.

• Use technology to set an example for others.

You will have the most success if you look at IT as something that enables you and your colleagues to be more effective and if you actively manage information technology.

Summary

Deciding how to allocate IT investments is far easier if management has a vision and a plan for IT, and if IT planning is closely coordinated with the firm's strategy. Many of the important IT investment decision criteria come from corporate strategy; an analysis of investments based solely on capital budgeting considerations is sterile and does not serve the firm well. A view from the perspective of corporate strategy is particularly important for investments in infrastructure, investments where indirect returns are possible, those that are a competitive necessity, where the nature of the application is strategic, and when an IT investment has the potential for transforming the organization. Management, strategy, and IT vision provide the context of the IT investment decision and have a major influence on how much value the firm receives from information technology.

CHAPTER TWELVE

Where IT Value is Found

s there value from investing in information technology? *Our first insight is that value depends on the type of IT investment.* Table 12-1 reviews IT investment types and comments on the kind of return one is likely to see. The table illustrates why it is difficult to prove there is value from IT investments, particularly if one wants to demonstrate a measurable financial return. For a number of investments, it is hard to identify the value returned because so many other factors influence outcomes. These investments may provide value in ways other than a clearly defined financial ROI.

Infrastructure investments may be necessary to undertake an IT initiative; a firm has to develop the networking technology in order to have an Intranet. Some infrastructure investment prepares for the future; it provides a platform to make it easier to develop applications of technology at some later date. Investments that are required will probably not show value; you make them because there is no choice and view the expenditure as a cost of doing business.

There are also investments where IT is the only option; there is no other feasible way to do the job. One could not make airline reservations with the kind of service provided by a CRS using manual methods, even if you could afford to hire enough agents to process reservations without technology. Here the objective is cost avoidance and better service. By rapidly expanding its base of technology the New York Stock Exchange was able to process many more trades, end the practice of closing the Exchange one day a week to catch up on processing, and control labor costs. All of these outcomes represent value returned to the Exchange, though it is difficult to identify an exact dollar amount or a rate of return.

Table 12-1
A Review of IT Investment Types

Type of Investment	Nature of Return	Comments	Upside
Infrastructure	Possible future benefits; hard to identify contribution	Support current business (may allow for future investments)	Little itself, but allows new programs
Required (no return) managerial control	Do not expect much of a return	A cost of business	Almost none
No other way to do the job	A return is very likely; may save labor or generate new revenue	Enable new task or process; provide better customer service and new products	Could gain more than forecast
Direct return from IT	The textbook case	Structured, cost/ benefit, and NPV appropriate	A little if you can build on the investment
Indirect returns	Very hard to identify	Potential for considerable return, but indirect benefits hard to estimate	Could be substantial future benefits
Competitive necessity	If you want to stay in this line of business, there is no choice; there may be no return except retaining market share	Need the system to compete in the business; what is the cost of not investing in technology?	Very little if you are following the industry

continued on next page

Table 12-1
continued from previous page

Strategic application	Hard to identify return; could influence corporate strategy	High risk-high potential; may be able to estimate return only after implementation	A high potential
Transforma-tional IT	IT a component of a change program; hard to identify specific returns tied to it	Must be combined with changes in management philosophy; good for fast response organization (risky to change structure, but high potential rewards)	A high potential

Investments that show a direct return are the classic textbook case. They are the ones most easily evaluated with traditional capital budgeting tools like net present value analysis. Indirect returns may arise from almost any investment; these returns have the potential to be quite high, though they, too, are hard to identify and trace back to an IT investment. In this book, our best example of indirect returns came from the airline strategy of deploying its reservations systems to travel agencies.

As firms invest heavily in information technology, they implement creative applications. Some of these applications are so compelling that competitors find they must invest in similar technology. Here, those who are not the "first movers" invest in IT to protect market share. The return from the investment may be simply maintaining the status quo with respect to market share, or being able to remain in a line of business.

Some IT investments are strategic in nature. An initiative may not start out that way, but at some point a manager recognizes a new opportunity. Order entry systems at Baxter and Braun Passot became strategic as each company began to build its strategy around information technology. Obviously this technology has provided significant value, but since it is so intertwined with strategy and other marketing programs, it is very hard to quantify its contribution.

One of the most exciting types of IT investments are applications to transform the organization. These investments are usually part of a larger change program; they enable new forms of organization like virtual and team-based structures. They make a contribution that is a part of the outcome of a general change effort.

Garbage Cans and Equations

We introduced a vision of the IT investment process as a giant garbage can. In the first such model, Cohen, March and Olson (1972) stated that "an organization is a collection of choices looking for problems, issues in which they might be aired, solutions looking for issues to which they might be the answer, and decision makers looking for work." The organization is a giant garbage can with issues, choices, problems, solutions, and decision makers all floating around together.

In the IT investment garbage can one can find actors and the technology to produce IT initiatives. This model illustrates the challenge of developing creative ideas for IT investment, and turning the investments into applications that produce value for the firm. A large number of factors must coalesce for the IT investment to accomplish its objectives and generate a return.

In general, how successful have organizations been in implementing their IT investments? A consulting firm has estimated, based on a survey of 360 companies, that in 1996, 73 percent of U.S. software projects were canceled, over budget, or late. At least less than 20 percent fall into the canceled category; the majority of the 73 percent are simply late or over budget (*ComputerWorld*, February 24, 1997).

The garbage can for IT value sends various projects down a pipe toward a "return on investment" spigot. The first thing they encounter is a filter called "conversion effectiveness." It is defined "as the effectiveness with which investments in IT are converted into useful outputs." Most approaches to evaluating IT investments assume a 100 percent conversion effectiveness; however, this probability can range from 0 to 1. It would be interesting go back in time to the initial decision to invest in the Air Traffic Control Modernization Project or the IRS Modernization effort to see if, looking at the objectives of the project, one could come up with a reasonable estimate of the probability for successful conversion. *The second major insight in our search for value is that not all IT investments are successfully converted into applications.*

The first observation, that a return depends on the type of IT investment, combined with the concept of conversion effectiveness leads to the *IT Investment Equation:*

P(Success/Return) = P(Return on Investment Type) × P(Conversion Success) where P means "probability of." This IT Investment Equation states that the probability of success in obtaining a return is equal to the probability of a return from an investment times the probability of successful conversion. It highlights the fact that value comes from the type of application and the organization's ability to convert the investment into a successful application.

What kind of return in an IT investment should the firm expect? We assume that managers will make some estimate of the return they expect to see from their IT investments. This return will depend on the type of investment and the particular circumstances of the investing firm. The *IT Value Equation* says that the expected return is the managers' dollar estimate of the benefits multiplied by the probability of that return multiplied by the probability of successful conversion.

$$
\begin{aligned}
\text{Expected Return} \; &= \; \text{Estimated Return} \times \text{P(Return)} \times \text{P(Conversion} \\
&\qquad \text{Success) or} \\
&= \; \text{Estimated Return} \times \text{P(Success/Return) or} \\
&= \; \text{Estimated return} \times \text{IT Investment Equation}
\end{aligned}
$$

You must weight the estimated return by the probability of obtaining the return and by the probability that you will convert the investment into a successful application. We suggested a number of strategies to increase the chances of successful conversion. The firm can follow traditional custom development approaches to implementation; it can supplement or even replace custom development through the use of packages, consultants and outsourcing agreements.

Reviewing the Evidence for Value

A third insight from the evidence is that some organizations have demonstrated value from their IT investments. Table 12-2 summarizes the main examples in this book.

In total we have looked at over 30 individual applications of IT or studies of multiple companies. In most of these cases the organizations appear to have received value from their IT investments. The most striking characteristic of the applications described in Table 12-2 is the lack of information on the return on investments; in most of the cases it is not possible to determine how much the organization has invested, so we cannot calculate an ROI. *We have found value, but not overwhelming evidence that this value represents a positive return on the firms' investments in IT.*

Table 12-2

Review of IT Value Examples

Investment	Results	Observations
Multiple Firms		
Valve industry study	Transactional IT associated with a positive return on investment	This study supports the contention that one cannot expect the same return from each type of IT investment
Airline computerized reservations systems	For the CRS vendors, investing in this technology led to highly profitable subsidiaries	We do not know the level of investment to calculate a return; the extremely high market value of the subsidiaries suggests a positive ROI
Econometric studies: 1. manufacturing firms 2. across 367 firms	1. No returns from IT 2. Very high rates of return from IT investment	Estimated return in second study seems too high based on experience
Commercial banks and risk management	A positive relationship found between functionality of risk management system and revenue from trading	This study suggests that it is not just investment in IT, but how well the firm converts the investment into system functionality
Study of 88 manufacturing firms from 1978 to 1984	IT capital is associated with intermediate business processes that, in turn, are associated with firm performance	The results support the argument that IT acts on firm-level performance through its impact on lower- level processes
Direct Return, No Other Way		
Merrill Lynch SPC system	Invest $3 million for less than two-year payback	Good example where we know investment and payback

continued on next page

Investment	Results	Observations
Chrysler EDI	Save $100 per car for systemwide savings of $220 million	We do not know investment, but suspect it was less than benefits
BZW trade system	Electronic trading system for correspondent brokerage firms	Led to increase in business of small trades for BZW; $1 million investment appears to have a positive return
Pacific Pride	Automated refueling depots provided customers with convenience and control	Allowed company to charge higher prices for fuel plus service
SABRE	No other way to handle reservations when jet travel began	System that American had to develop became a competitive advantage for the airline
Air Traffic Control system	No way to handle today's volume of flights manually	The federal government made the investment for the system; the benefits accrue to flying public, airlines, private aviation (their total value has not been estimated)
Federal Express	Investment in IT the only reasonable way to track packages; today FedEx claims to invest $1 billion a year in technology to improve service and productivity	Some savings are likely for customer service; new investment for productivity enhancement should be able to show direct return; customer service investments more difficult to evaluate
VeriFone and credit card companies	Systems to improve verification; IT the only way to handle today's volume of business	Easy to calculate benefits to merchant from VeriFone products; for Visa, MasterCard, Amex, Discover, etc., technology enables increasing volume of transactions; the return is removing constraints on growth

continued on next page

Table 12-2
continued from previous page

Investment	Results	Observations
Indirect Returns		
CRS in travel agencies	Study found substantial, indirect, nonfee performance associated with having a vendor airline's CRS in a travel agency	Do not know how much the airlines invested in this technology to calculate a return
American Hospital Supply-Baxter-Allegiance	Thirty years of IT investment, changing the nature of firm's strategy and products	Do not know total investment; extensive use of IT suggests considerable indirect benefits from this investment
Zeta Corporation	Implementation of Notes for call tracking resulted in substantial changes in the nature of customer service	There was no attempt to value the indirect benefits from the application, nor do we know the initial investment
Otis	Presence on the Web does not appear to generate revenues	Provides substantial information to public, shareholders, contractors; benefits appear to be indirect
Infrastructure		
Singapore networking	Substantial movement of commerce to electronic transactions processing; stimulated "intelligent island" vision	A government-sponsored initiative that was transferred at least partially to the private sector; infrastructure seen as an investment on which to build
Study of 25 companies (Weill 1990)	Infrastructure provides a base for future applications; can amount to 40 percent + of IT budget	The return on infrastructure investment is likely to take place in the future

continued on next page

Investment	Results	Observations
Intranets	Provide an in-house Web and encourage users to develop pages and applications	An opportunity to move to a common interface among systems, reduce paper, and increase access to information; very difficult to measure return except for reduced publishing costs

Strategic Technology

Investment	Results	Observations
Rosenbluth	Invested up to half of pretax profits in IT; became a key in growth strategy	Built on airline CRS infrastructure to offer better products to clients
Braun Passot	Began with Minitel and grew to PC applications	Built on existing infrastructure; IT demonstrated value, and management built more of its strategy around it
State Street Bank	Emphasized financial services for funds; IT enabled it to capture significant market share	Technology became a part of strategy, as it proved successful in serving clients
H. E. Butt	History of IT investment to reduce costs and focus on low-price strategy	EDI, CRP, ECR all contribute to lower costs; the total IT investment has become a part of HEB's strategy to compete
ATM studies	1. There was little advantage from ATMs except where the bank belonged to the major ATM network 2. First movers appeared to obtain and sustain an advantage in market share and income	ATMs are a necessity, especially membership in a network

continued on next page

Table 12-2
continued from previous page

Investment	Results	Observations
Southwest Airlines CRS	A Web interface for making reservations; a necessity for competition	Southwest will not pay booking fees to CRS vendors, so it must find alternative channels to make a reservation
UPS, FedEx	IT as a strategy becomes a basis for competition	Customers benefit as business is redefined from packages to packages plus information about them

Transformational IT

Investment	Results	Observations
Frito-Lay	Began with $40 million for hand-held computer; evolved to change operations and management	Frito-Lay created a hybrid organization with old and new features; it has decentralized decision making to lower levels of the firm through technology
Mrs. Fields Cookies	Technology used for all aspects of control, both financial and product quality	A dual structure that is hierarchical for sales and flat for financial control
VeriFone	"Appropriate" technology facilitates communications and information sharing	VeriFone is a true virtual organization
Calyx and Corolla	Technology coordinates different virtual components	C&C built a new organization by snapping together different components, several of which are virtual
Oticon	The company developed technology to facilitate flexible work assignments and a team-based organization	Technology is the glue that holds Oticon's teams together; it makes it possible to coordinate work and track progress

Do these results mean that firms have made poor investment decisions? Is the high level of investment in IT for the economy as a whole a mistake? We have seen examples where investments in IT are associated with a measurable financial return, like the Merrill Lynch securities processing system. The indirect benefits from airline CRS deployment in travel agencies also looks like a positive return. The CRS vendor airlines' reservations subsidiaries are highly profitable; the indirect benefits we found represent an additional return. The Chrysler EDI and JIT applications produced estimated savings that seem large enough to exceed any reasonable level of IT investment required to realize them. VeriFone presents a good case that the technology it sells for transactions authorization provides its customers with a return on their investment. Pacific Pride appears to have used IT successfully to charge above average prices for fuel sold to commercial fleets.

The examples discussed here demonstrate that one does not expect the same kind of return and value from every IT investment. Sometimes management will allocate resources to investments that are expected to show a direct return. In other instances, the decision to invest will be made to retain market share in a competitive industry. Still other applications may advance corporate strategy or enable the organization to transform its structure. The return from these investments is confounded with the return from the firm's strategy or its change program.

I believe the examples in this book demonstrate value from investing in information technology. Value is not just an easily measured dollar return on invested capital. Value comes from investments that contribute to an organization's strategy, through indirect returns, by meeting the competition and protecting market share, and in a variety of ways illustrated by the firms we have discussed.

In Chapter 1, I stated a personal belief that the cumulative impact of investments in information technology exceed the sum of their individual contributions (see Figure 1-1). Applications of IT interact with each other, creating new benefits and opportunities. IT becomes woven into the fabric of the organization, and continued innovation becomes a part of doing business. Infrastructure is in place to quickly take advantage of new opportunities and respond to competitive threats.

Decision makers need to realize that value has many different definitions when looking at IT investments, and it is not always easy to estimate or measure. This complex investment problem means that managers have to gather information and consider a variety of factors in making their decisions about allocating resources to IT. Following that allocation, they have to monitor carefully the conversion of the investment into an IT application. Creating value through IT investments is a major challenge, one that requires significant management effort and attention.

Making the Investment

There is evidence of value from investing in information technology. Many managers must have come to this conclusion if it is true that half of U.S. capital investment today is for technology. Because IT is so pervasive and is used in so many different ways, it may not always be possible to associate a particular IT initiative with a stream of revenue or cost savings. It would appear that management is committed to investing in IT; the issue is how to allocate scarce investment dollars among competing proposals for technology.

We advocated a broad approach to this resource allocation decision. In particular, it is important for the organization to have a strategy, plan, and vision for IT. In some of the examples, it is clear that the firm's overall strategy was more important in deciding to invest in IT than was the economic analysis for the investment.

To help make IT investment decisions, we proposed that the decision-making body, a steering committee of some kind, look at very specific information. It should examine this information for the firm's IT investment portfolio to allow for comparisons among past, current, and proposed applications. The information to examine, which can easily be presented on a spreadsheet, includes the following:

The type of the investment, for example, required, infrastructure, competitive, etc.

The estimated investment required, the cost of the initiative

The estimated return: This is an estimate, taking into account the type of investment—for example, there may be no return from a required application

The probability of a return

The probability of successful conversion

The S/R index (the product of the two probabilities above)

The expected value from the investment: the estimated return times the probability of obtaining that return times the probability of conversion success

The results of applying a capital budgeting model if one is used

An estimate of the possible upside from the investment.

The traditional capital budgeting model is net present value, which discounts revenues and costs to a single point in time for comparison purposes. In some instances, we saw that an IT investment may look more like an option when there is a question of timing on when to make the investment, or when a current investment sets the stage for a follow-on project. In these instances, one can carefully use an options pricing model, remaining aware that IT projects are not completely analogous to a financial option.

It is not possible to provide a formula for combining all of the above-mentioned criteria to come up with a decision. Some of the items in the spreadsheet are quantitative and others are qualitative. *The recommended information for use in making IT investment decisions provides a variety of measures for managers to consider, along with the firm's overall strategy and vision for technology, in deciding how to allocate resources to investments in information technology.*

Conclusion

The purpose of this book was to

1. present a perspective on the nature of the return from investing in IT.

    • There are different types of IT investments, each having a different pattern of potential returns.

2. demonstrate that there have been and should continue to be benefits from IT investments: There is value to be found in information technology.

    • Examples throughout this book provide evidence of value from IT, but only a few cases allow us to quantify value and compare it with investment costs to develop an ROI figure.

3. suggest ways to look for both the obvious and the more subtle value from IT.

    • The examples show a wide variety of ways in which IT can provide value, including indirect returns, strategic applications where the firm's strategy and technology become intertwined, and transformational technology where management develops applications as a part of a program to make major changes in the organization.

4. Make recommendations on how to evaluate investments in technology when they are proposed.

   • We have suggested a decision process and information for making the IT investment decision that includes economic and noneconomic factors, stressing the importance of corporate strategy and vision and focusing on the portfolio of IT investment opportunities.

Organizations that flourish in the future will make wise decisions about investments in information technology and will successfully convert those investments into applications. Managers in these firms view IT as an asset and believe that their IT investments produce value for the firm. These managers have a strategy and vision for technology, and they actively manage IT. They do not have to search for value from information technology, they create it.

REFERENCES

Applegate, L. "Frito-Lay, Inc.: A Strategic Transition (A) (Updated)." Boston, Harvard Business School, 1993.

Banker, R., and R. Kauffman. "Strategic Contributions of Information Technology: An Empirical Study of ATM Networks." *Proceedings of the Ninth International Conference on Information Systems*. Minneapolis, 1988.

Barua, A., C. Kriebel, and T. Mukhopadhyay. "Information Technologies and Business Value: An Analytic and Empirical Investigation." *Information Systems Research* 6 (March 1995): pp. 3-23.

Benaroch, M., and R. Kauffman. "A Case for Using Options Pricing Analysis to Evaluate Information Technology Project Investments." *Information Systems Research* (forthcoming).

Bjorn-Andersen, N. and J Turner. "Creating the 21st Century Organization: The Metamorphosis of Oticon." Paper presented at the IFSP Working Group 8-2 Conference. Ann Arbor, MI, August 1994.

Black, F., and M. Scholes. "The Pricing of Options and Corporate Liabilities." *Journal of Political Economy* 81 (May-June 1973): 637-54.

Broadbent, M., P. Weill, T. O'Brien, and B. Neo. "Firm Context and Patterns of IT Infrastructure Capability." *Proceedings of the 17th International Conference on Information Systems*. Cleveland, 1996.

Brynjolfsson, E. "The Productivity Paradox of Information Technology." *Communications of the ACM* 35 (Dec. 1993): 66-77.

Brynjolfsson, E. "The Contribution of Information Technology to Consumer Welfare." *Information Systems Research* 8 (September 1996): 281-300.

Brynjolfsson, E., and L. Hitt. "Is Information Systems Spending Productive? New Evidence and New Results." *Proceedings of the 14th International Conference on Information Systems.* Orlando, 1993.

————. "Paradox Lost? Firm-level Evidence on the Returns to Information Systems Spending." *Management Science* 42 (April 1996): 541-58.

Clark, T., and D. Croson. "H. E. Butt Grocery Company: A Leader in ECR Implementation." Boston, Harvard Business School, 1994.

Clemons, E. "MAC-A Venture in Shared ATM Networks." *JMIS* 7 (Summer 1990): 5-25.

Clemons, E., and M. Row. "Information Technology at Rosenbluth Travel." *JMIS* 8 (Fall 1991): 53-79.

Clemons, E., and B. Weber. "Barclays de Zoete Wedd's TRADE System: 1988-1993." New York, Stern School of Business, NYU, 1996.

Cohen, M., J. March, and J. Olsen. "A Garbage Can Model of Organizational Choice." *Administrative Science Quarterly* 17 (1972): 1-18.

Copeland. D. and J. McKenney. "Airline Reservations Systems: Lessons from History." *MIS Quarterly* 12 (Sept 1988): 353-70.

Davenport, T. H., R. Eccles, and L. Prusak. "Information Politics." *Sloan Management Review* 34 (Fall 1992): 53-65.

Dos Santos, B. "Justifying Investments in New Information Technologies." *JMIS* 7 (Spring 1991): 71-90.

Dos Santos, B., and K. Peffers. "Rewards to Investors in Innovative Information Technology Applications: First Movers and Early Followers in ATMs." *Organization Science* 6 (May-June 1995): 241-59.

Duliba, Katherine. "The Business Value of Information Technology Investment in International Banking: A Focus on Global Risk Management Technology." Unpublished Ph.D. dissertation. Stern School of Business, NYU, 1998.

Duliba, K., R. Kauffman, and H. Lucas, Jr. "Appropriability and the Indirect Value of CRS Ownership in the Airline Industry." Working paper. New York: Stern School of Business, NYU, 1997.

Earl, M. and D. Feeny. "Is Your CIO Adding Value?" *Sloan Management Review* 35 (Spring 1994): 11-20.

Ewusi-Mensah, K. "Critical Issues in Abandoned Information Systems Development Projects." *Communications of the ACM* 40 (September 1997): 74-80.

Francalanci, C. "State Street Boston Corporation: Leading with Information Technology." Boston, Harvard Business School, 1995.

Galal, H. "VeriFone: The Transaction Automation Company (A)." Boston, Harvard Business School, 1995.

Garud, R., and H. C. Lucas, Jr. "Virtual Organizations: What You See May Not Be What You Get." Working paper. New York, Stern School of Business, NYU, 1997.

Gibb, W. "Taking Computers to Task." *Scientific American* (July 1997): 82-9.

Jelassi, T., and O. Fignon. "Competing Through EDI at Braun Passot: Achievements in France and Ambitions for the Single European Market." *MIS Quarterly* 18 (December 1994): 337-52.

Kambil, A., J. Henderson, and H. Mohsenzadeh. "Strategic Management of Information Technology Investments: An Options Perspective." In *Strategic Information Technology Management,* R. Banker, R. Kauffman, and M. Mahmood (eds.), Harrisburg, Pa.: Idea Group Publishing, 1993, 161-78.

King, J., and B. Konsynski. "Singapore TradeNet: A Tale of One City." Boston, Harvard Business School, 1994.

Kumaraswamy, A. "A Real Options Perspective of Firms' R&D Investments." Unpublished Ph.D. dissertation, Stern School of Business, NYU, 1996.

Loveman, G. W. "An Assessment of the Productivity Impact on Information Technologies." In *Information Technology and the Corporation of the 1990s: Research Studies,* T. J. Allen and M. S. Scott Morton (eds.). Cambridge, Mass.: MIT Press, 1994.

Lucas, H. C., Jr. *The T-Form Organization: Using Technology to Design Organizations for the 21st Century.* San Francisco: Jossey-Bass, 1996.

Lucas, H. C., Jr. *Information Technology for Management* (6th ed.). New York: McGraw-Hill, 1997.

Marshall, C. "Baxter International: On Call as Soon as Possible?" Boston, Harvard Business School, 1995.

Montealegre, R., and H. J. Nelson, "BAE Automated Systems (A): Denver International Airport Baggage-handling System." Boston, Harvard Business School Press, 1996.

Mukhopadhyay, T., S. Kekre, and S. Kalathur. "Business Value of Information Technology: A Study of Electronic Data Interchange." *MIS Quarterly* 19 (June 1995): 137-56.

Nault, B., and A. Dexter. "Added Value and Pricing with Information Technology." *MIS Quarterly* 19 (December 1995): 449-64.

Neo, B., J. King, and L. Applegate. "Singapore TradeNet: The Tale Continues." Boston, Harvard Business School, 1995.

Orlikowski, W. "Improvising Organizational Transformation Over Time: A Situated Change Perspective" *Information Systems Research* 7 (March 1996): 63-92.

Short, J., and N. Venkatraman. "Beyond Business Process Redesign: Redefining Baxter's Business Network." *Sloan Management Review* 34 (Fall 1992): 7-21.

Teo, H., B. Tan, and K. Wei. "Organizational Transformation Using Electronic Data Interchange: The Case of TradeNet in Singapore." *JMIS* 13 (1997): 139-65.

Venkatraman, N., and A. Zaheer. "Electronic Integration and Strategic Advantage: A Quasi-Experimental Study in the Insurance Industry." *Information Systems Research* 1 (December 1990): 377-93.

Weill, P. *Do Computers Pay Off?* Washington, D.C.: ICIT Press, 1990.

Weill, P. "The Role and Value of IT Infrastructure: Some Empirical Observations." In *Strategic Information Technology Management: Perspectives on Organizational Growth and Competitive Advantage,* M. Khosrowpour and M. Mahmood (eds.). Harrisburg: Idea Group Publishing, 1993, pp. 547-72.

Weill, P., M. Broadbent, and C. Butler. "Exploring How Firms View IT Infrastructure." Melbourne, Australia: Melbourne Business School, 1996.

INDEX